candy

This book belongs to:

●---

●---

Coloring book

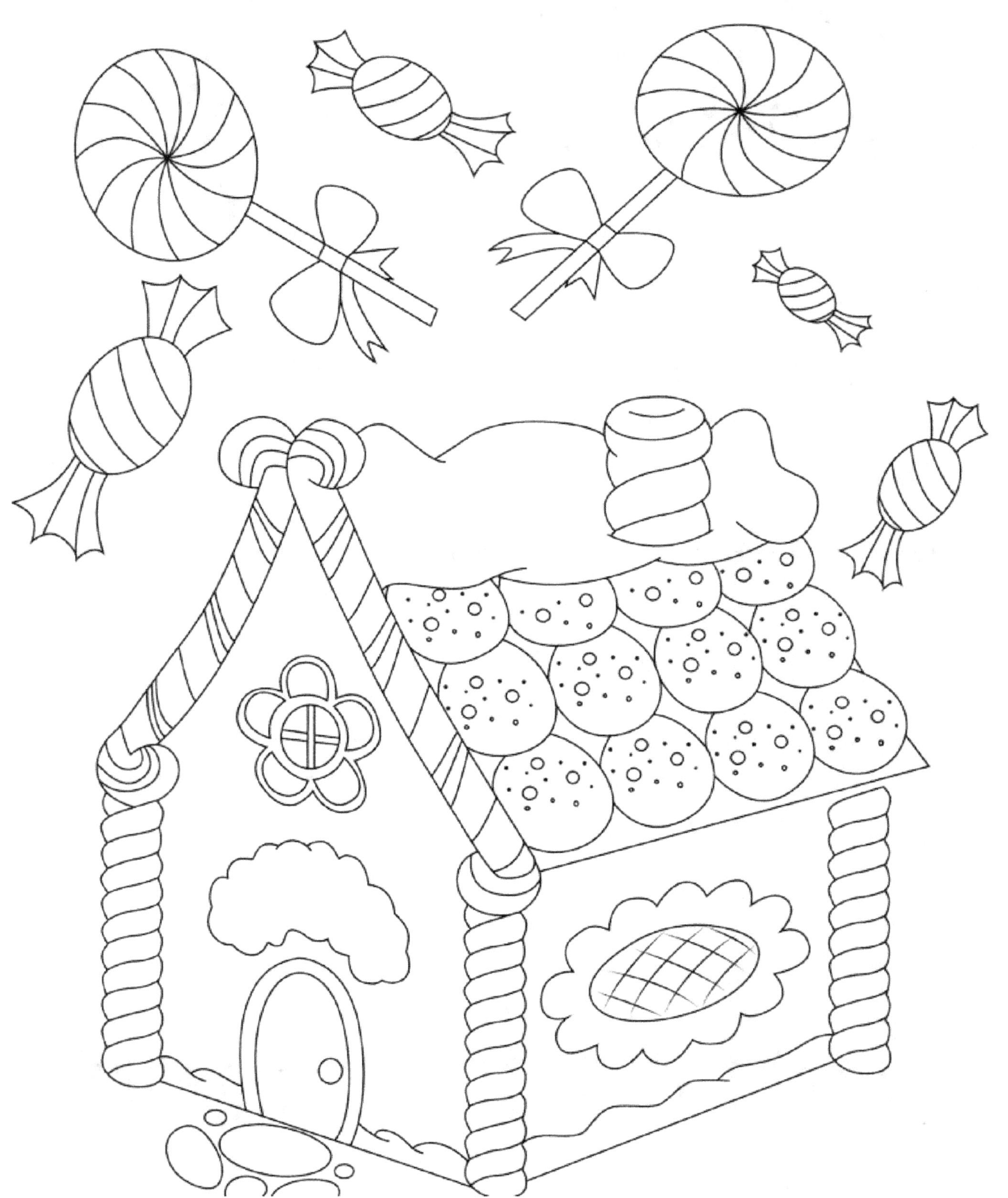

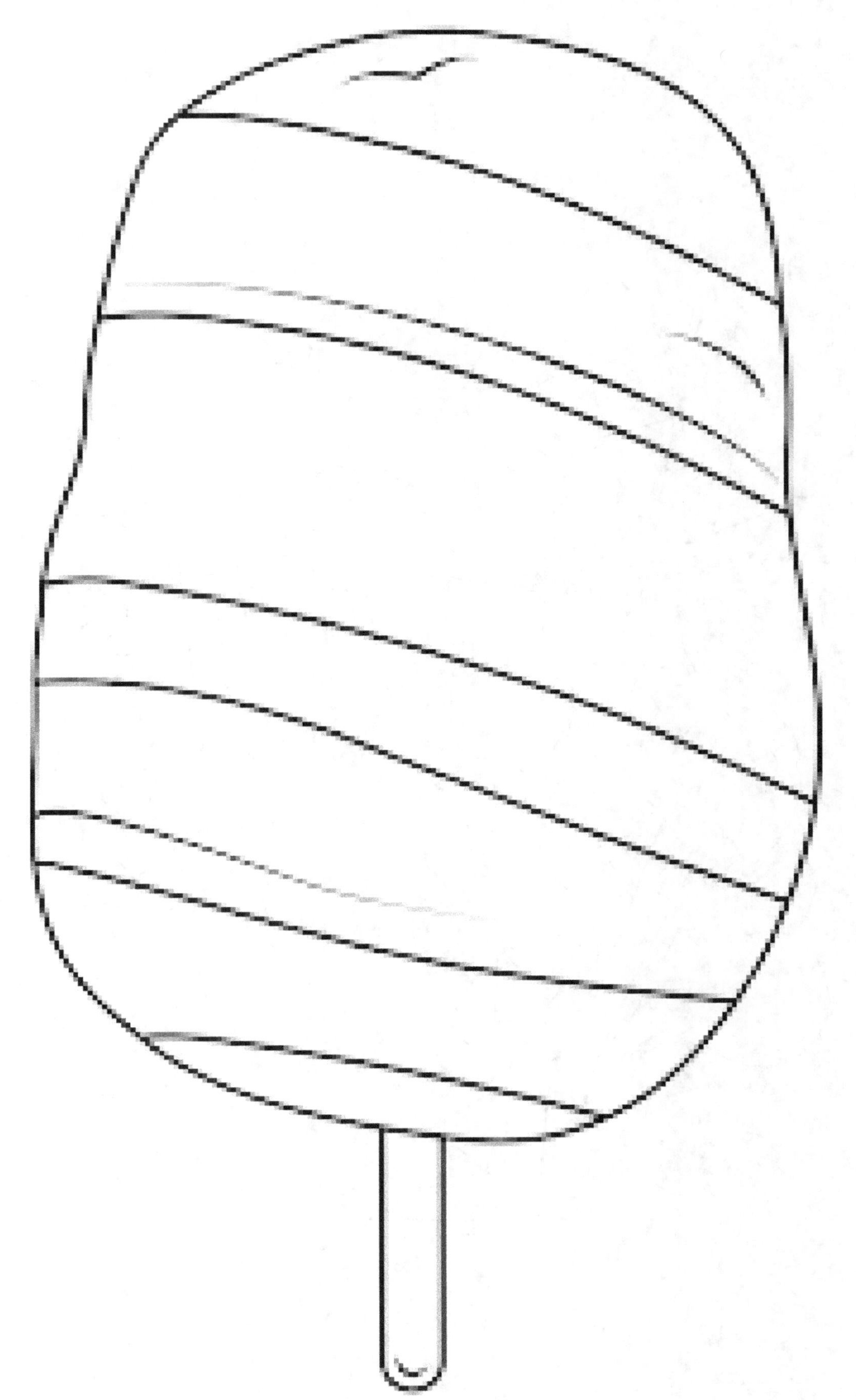

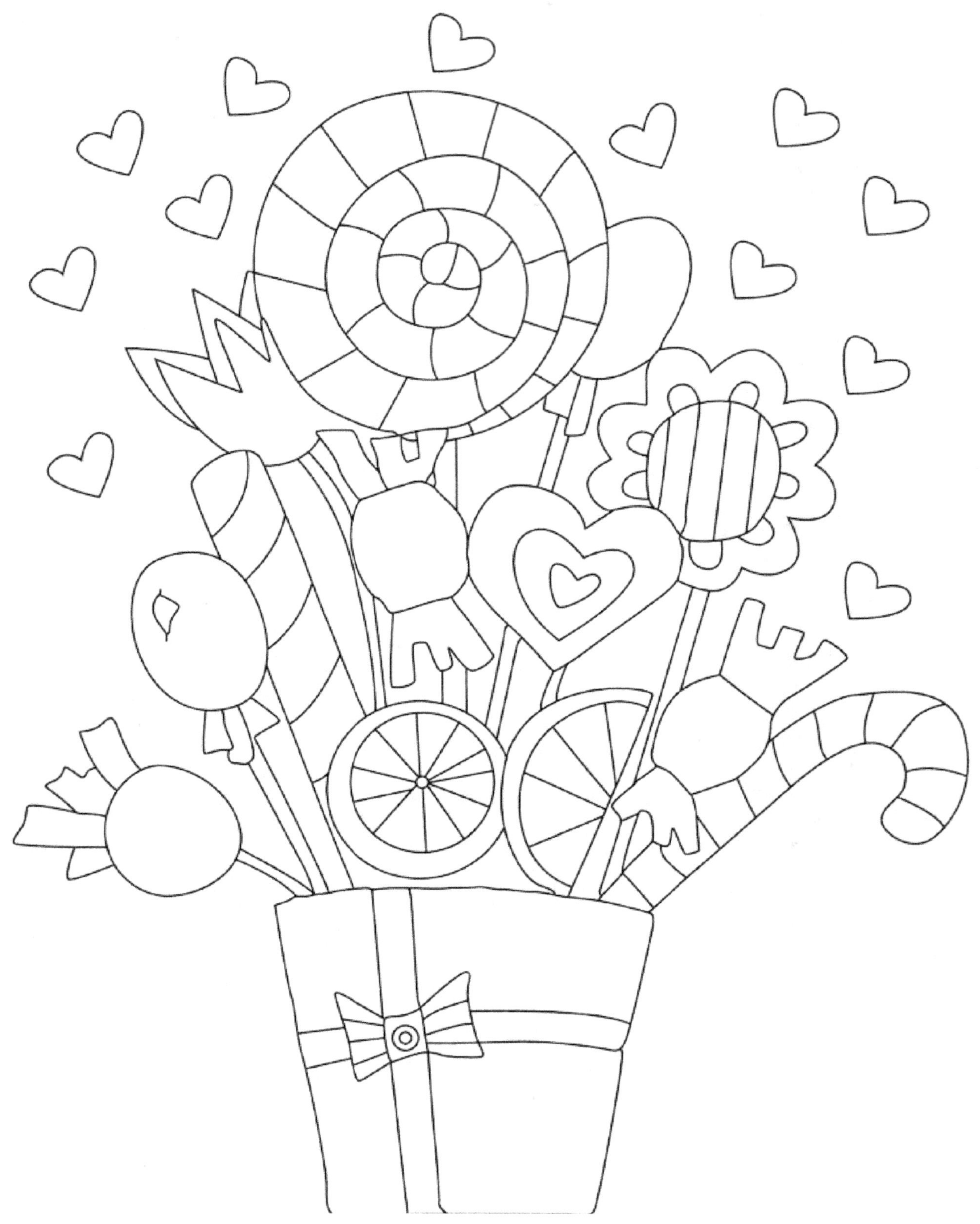

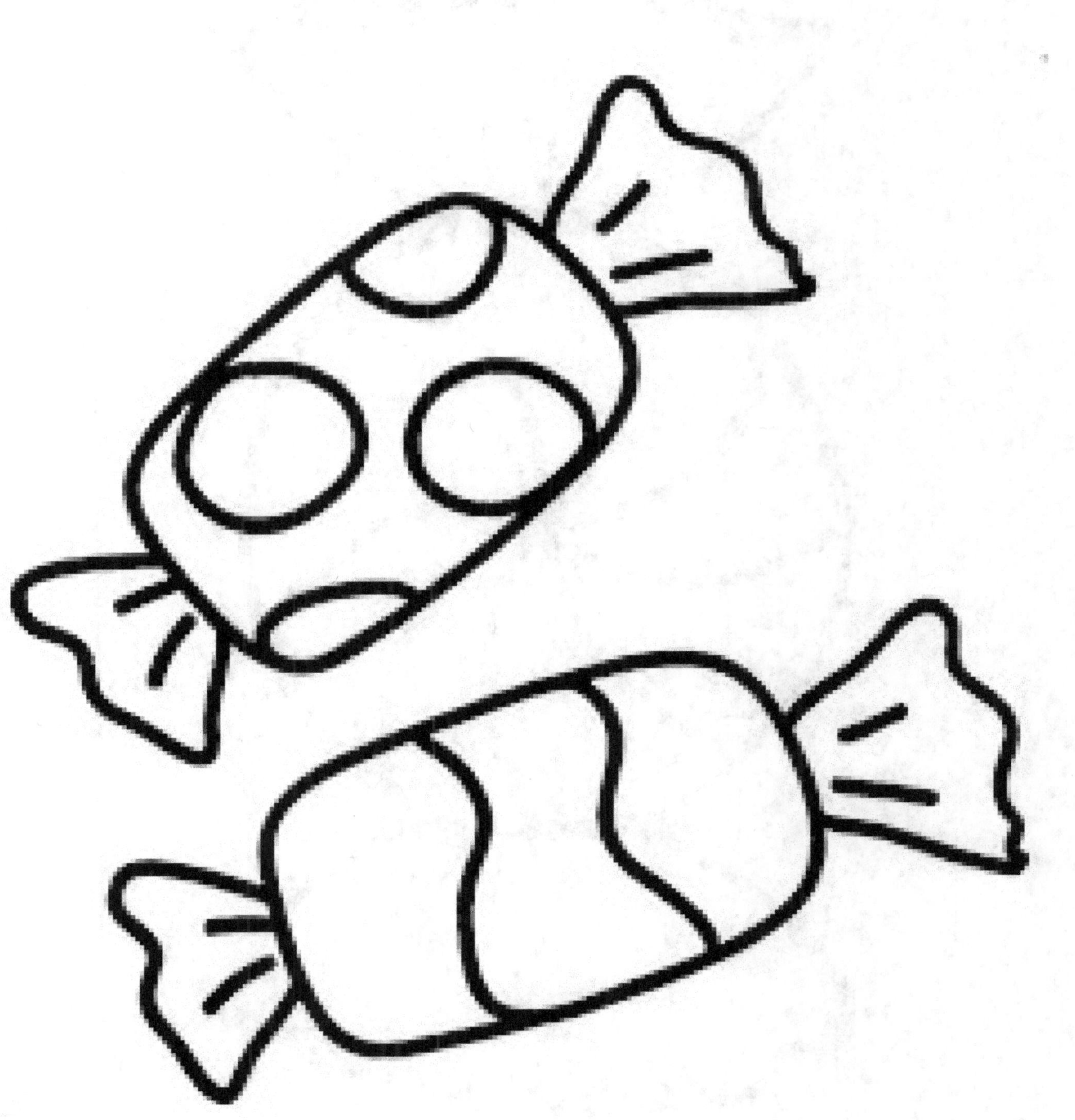

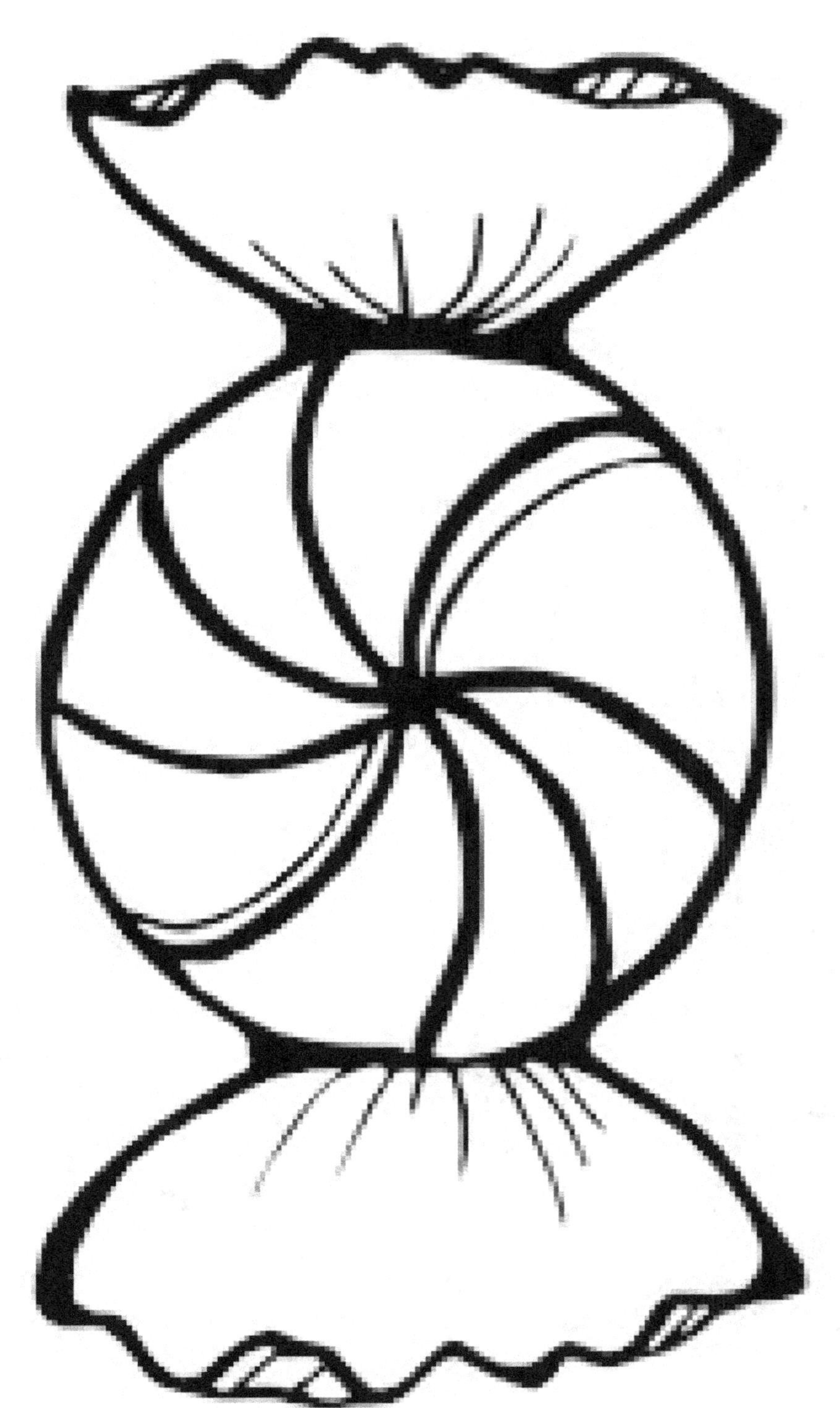

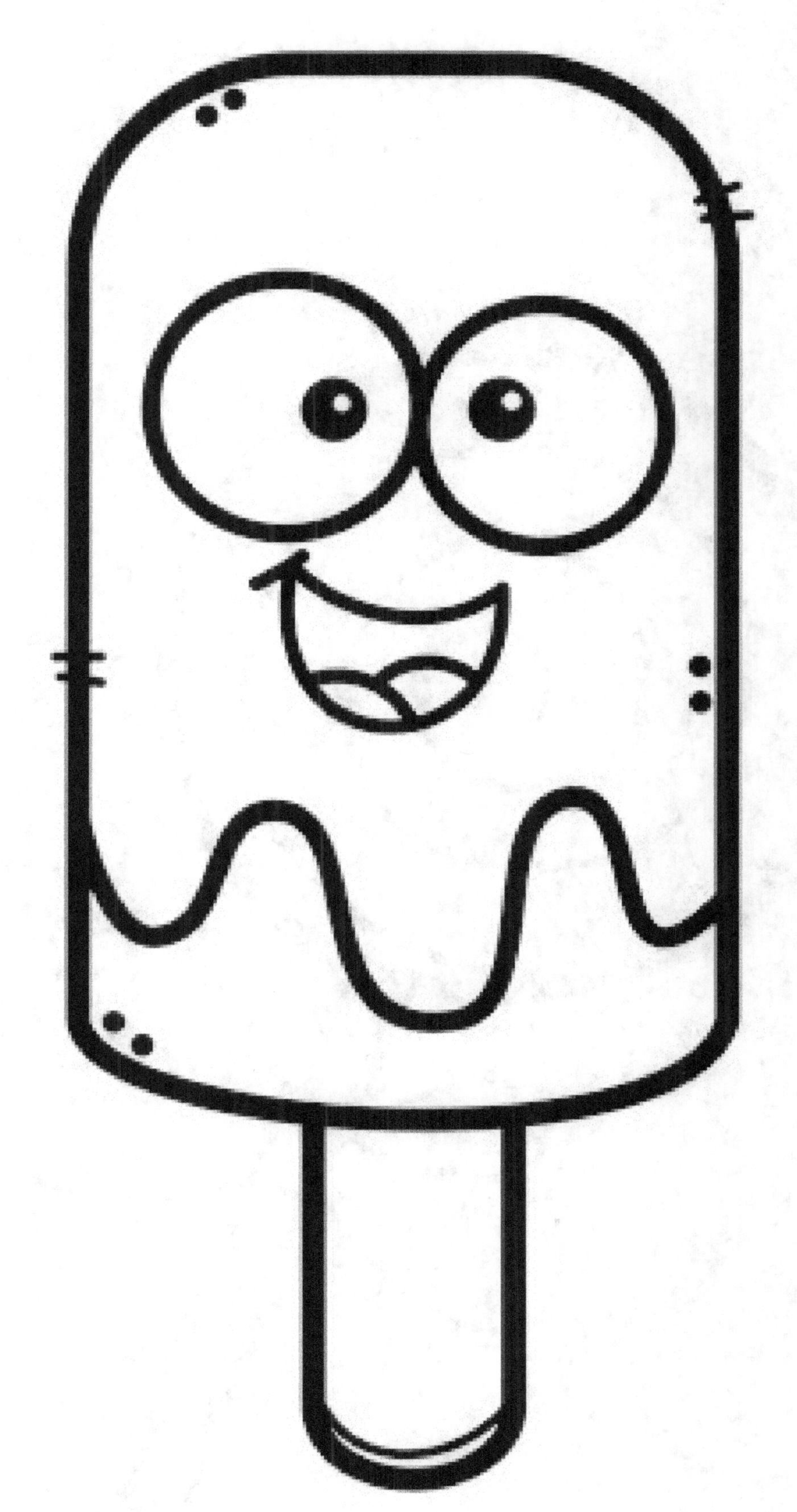

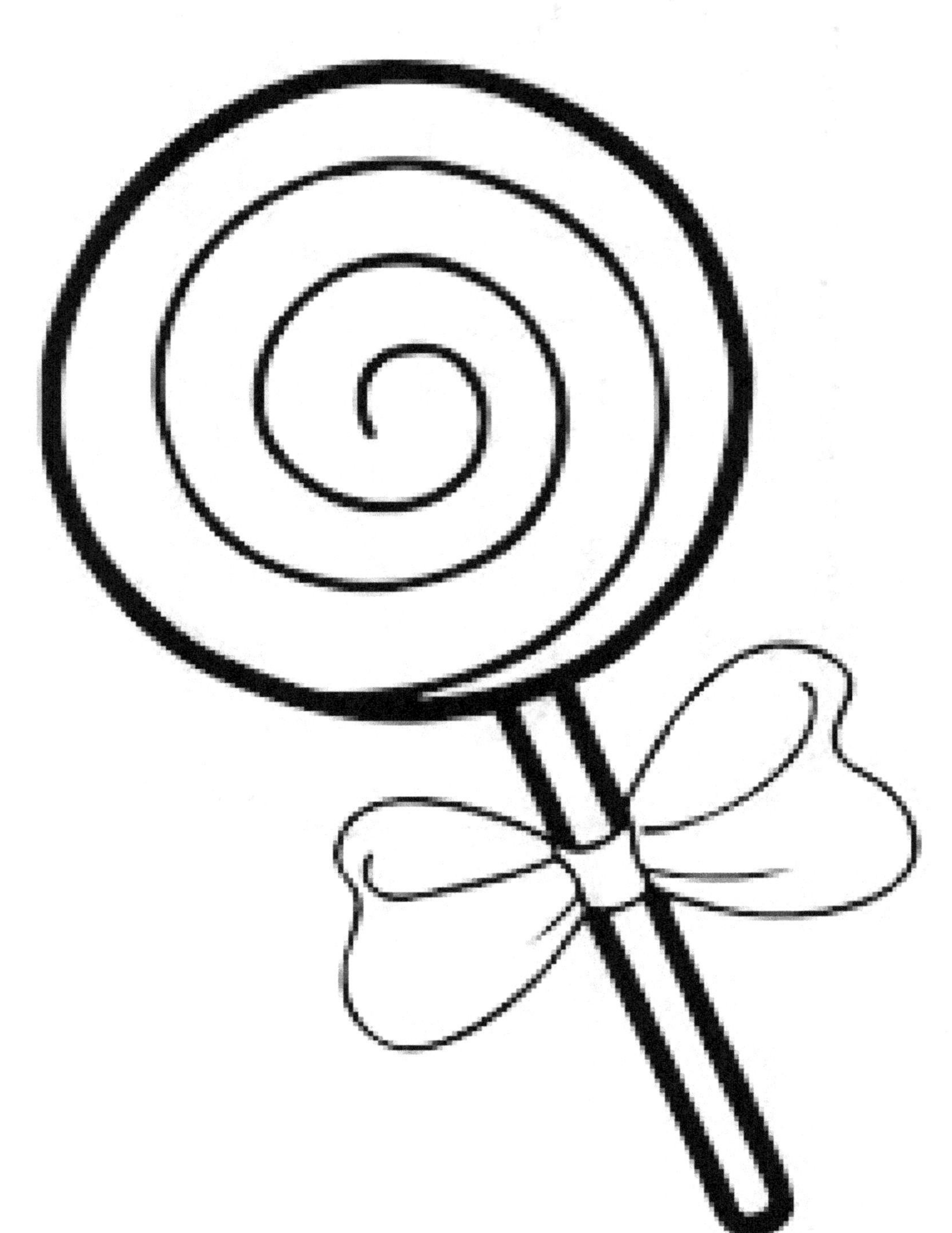

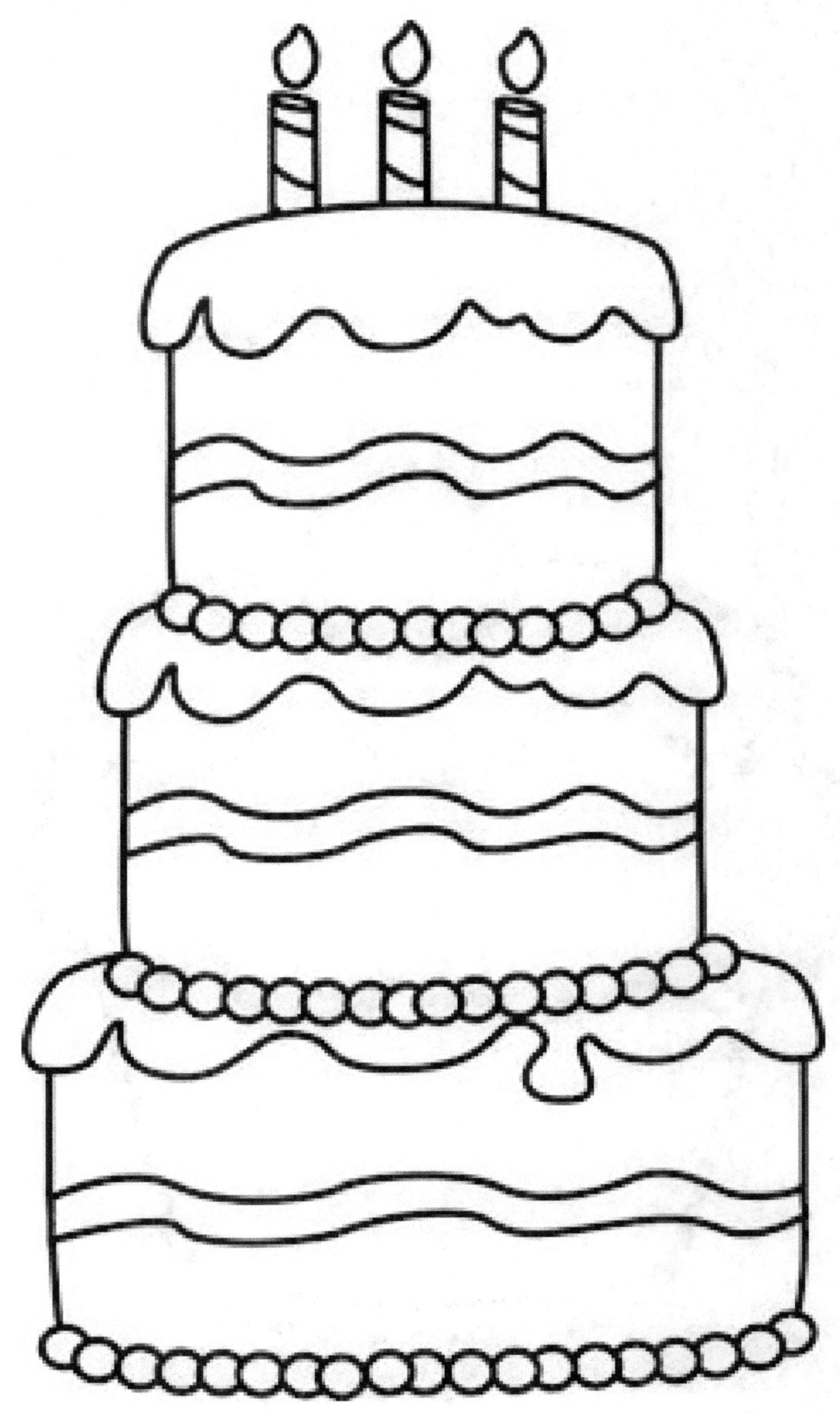

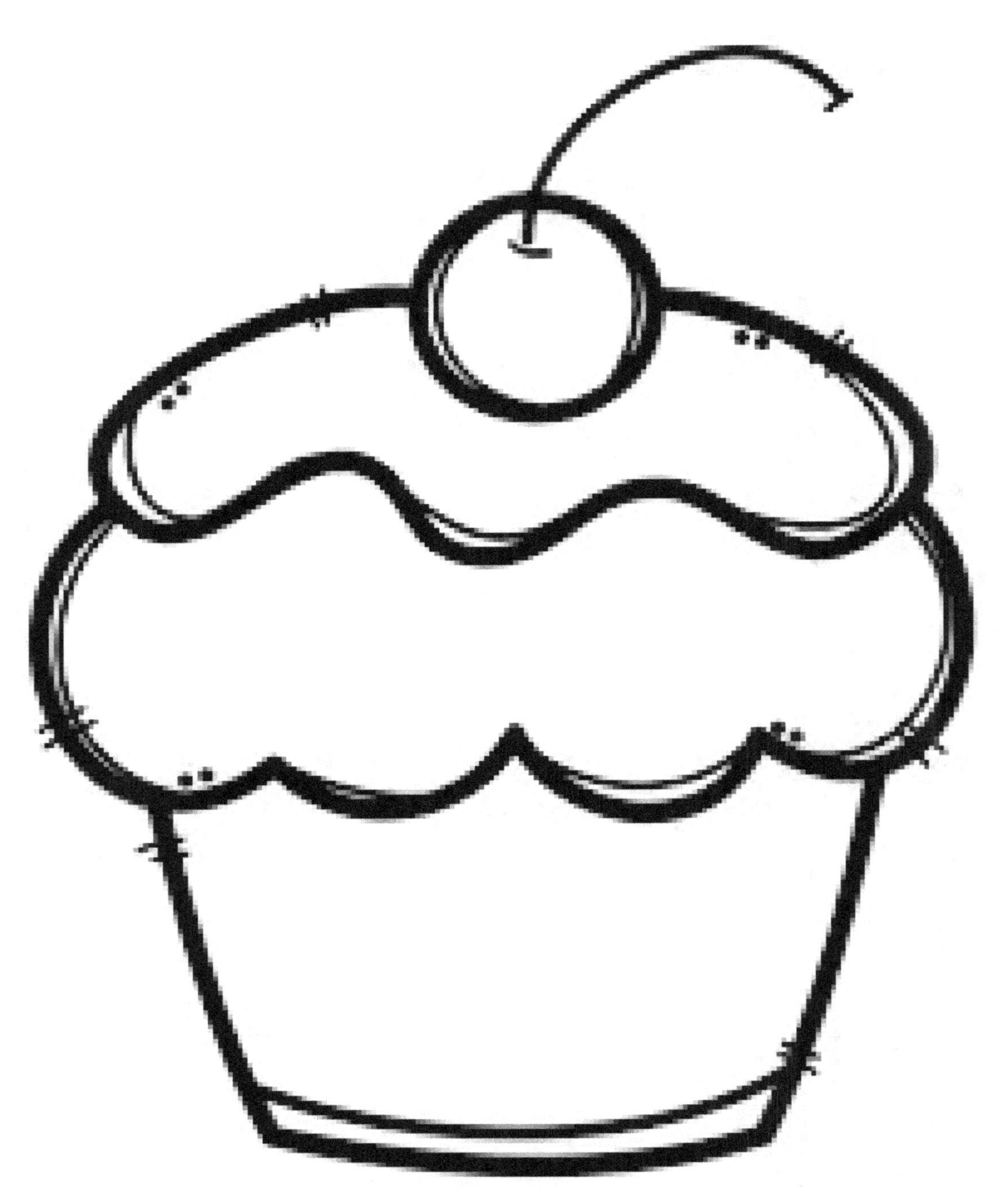

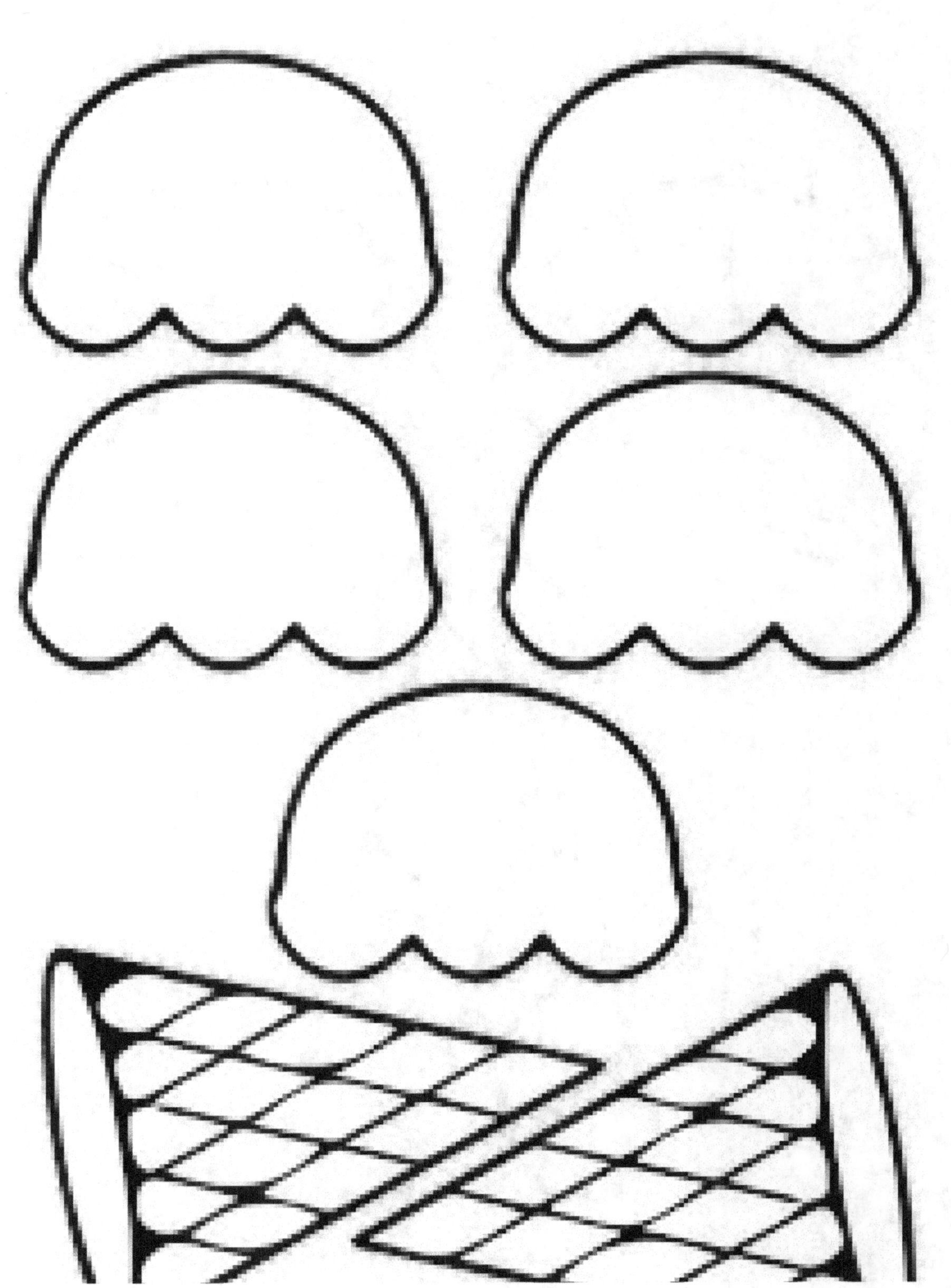

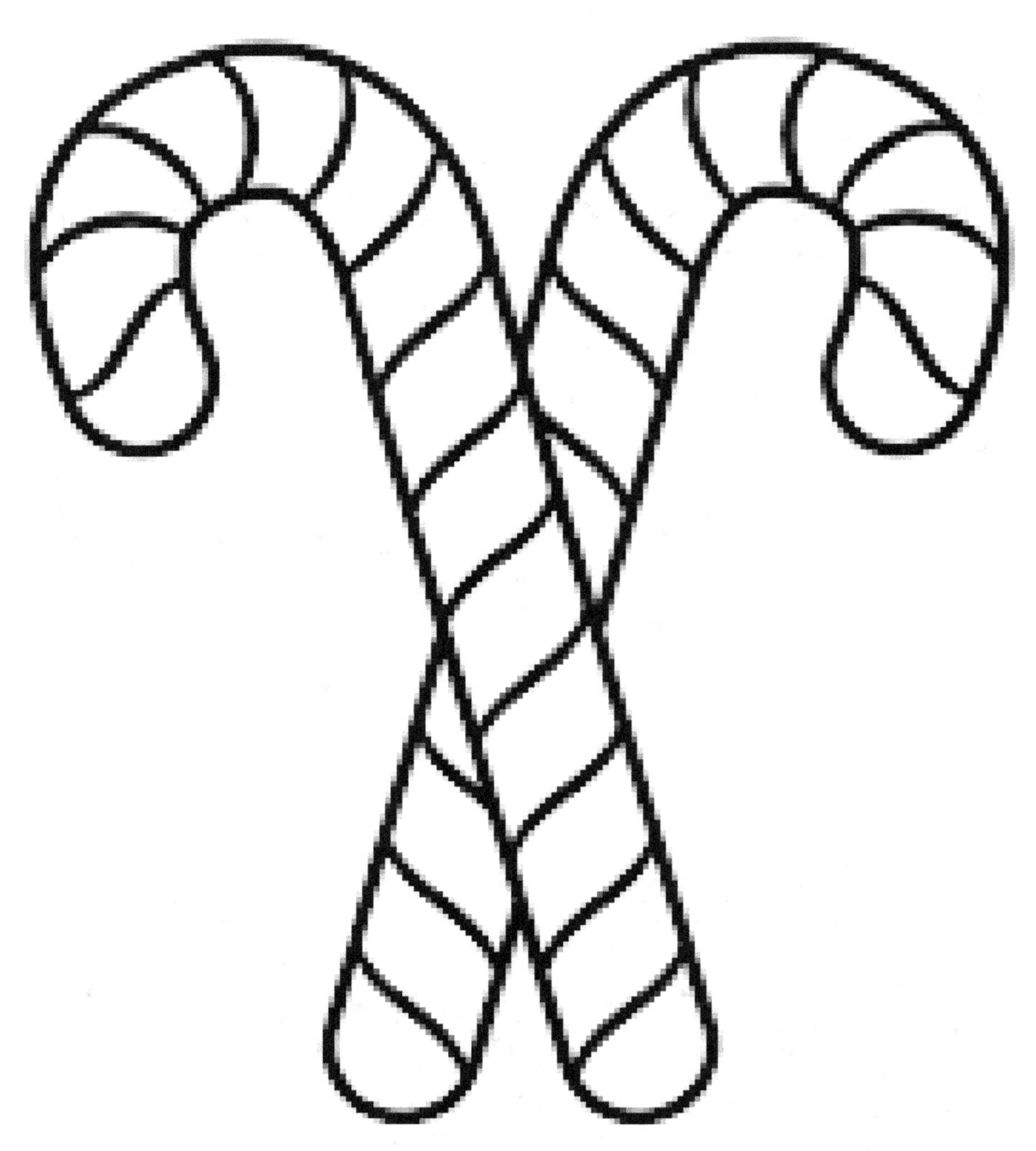

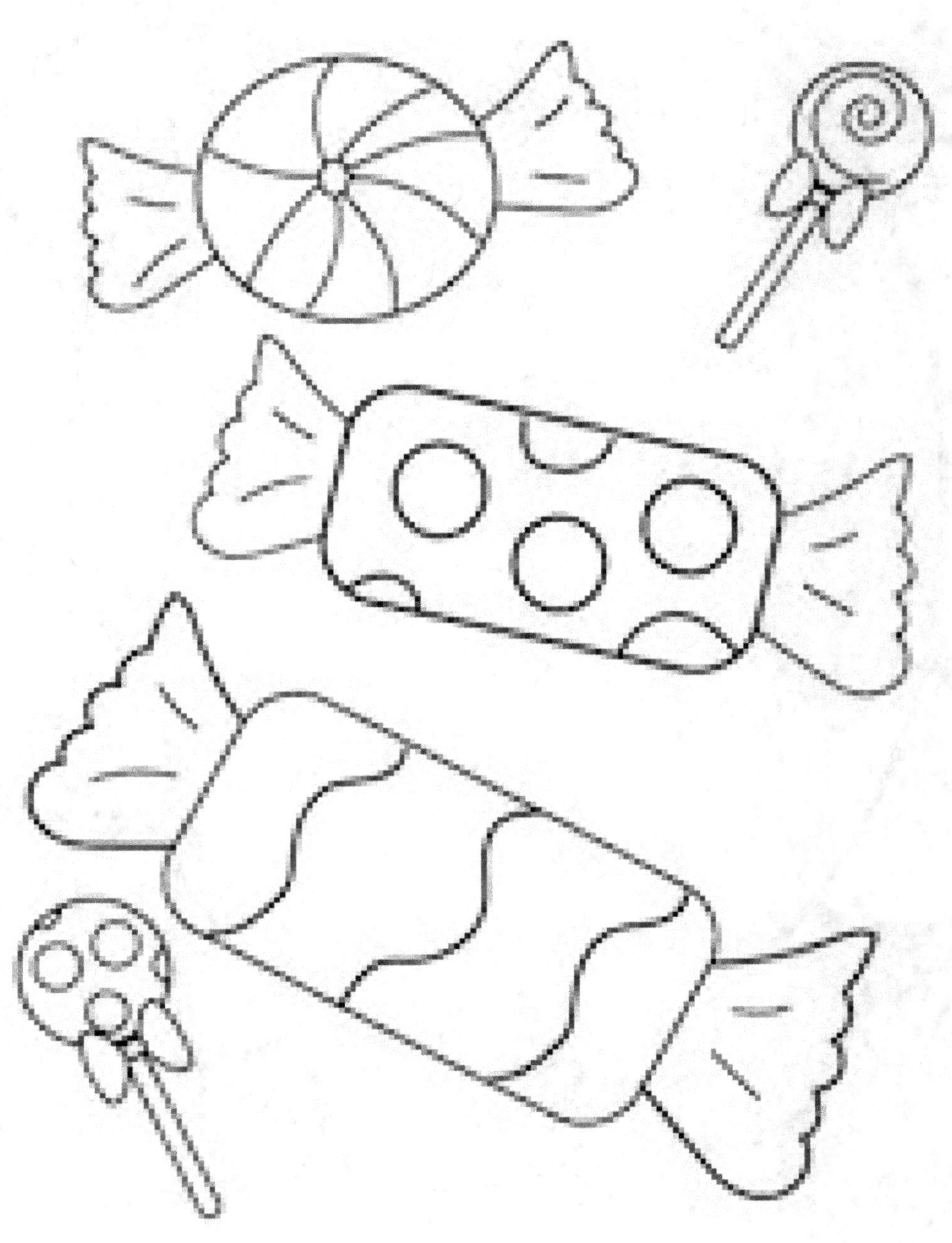

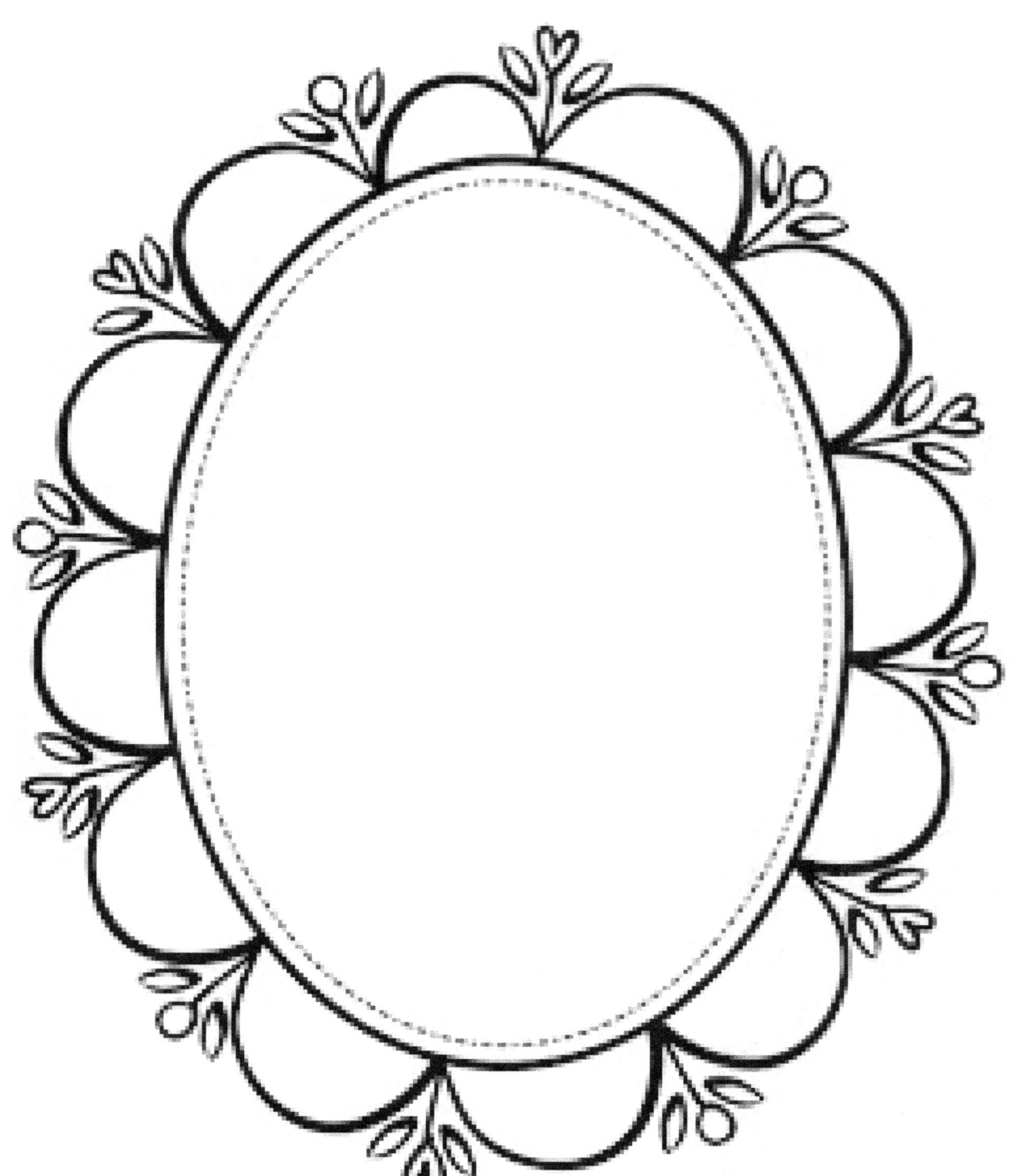

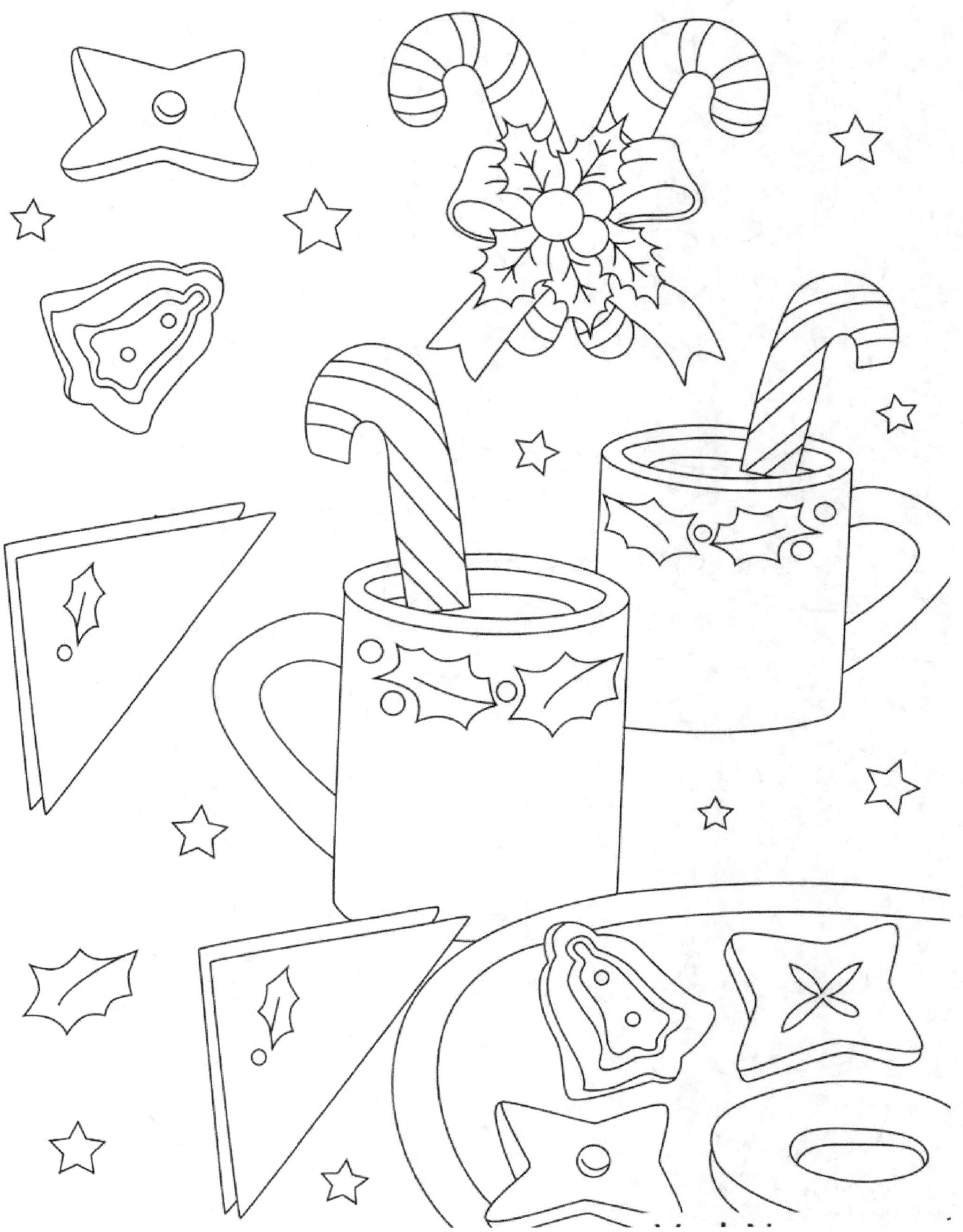

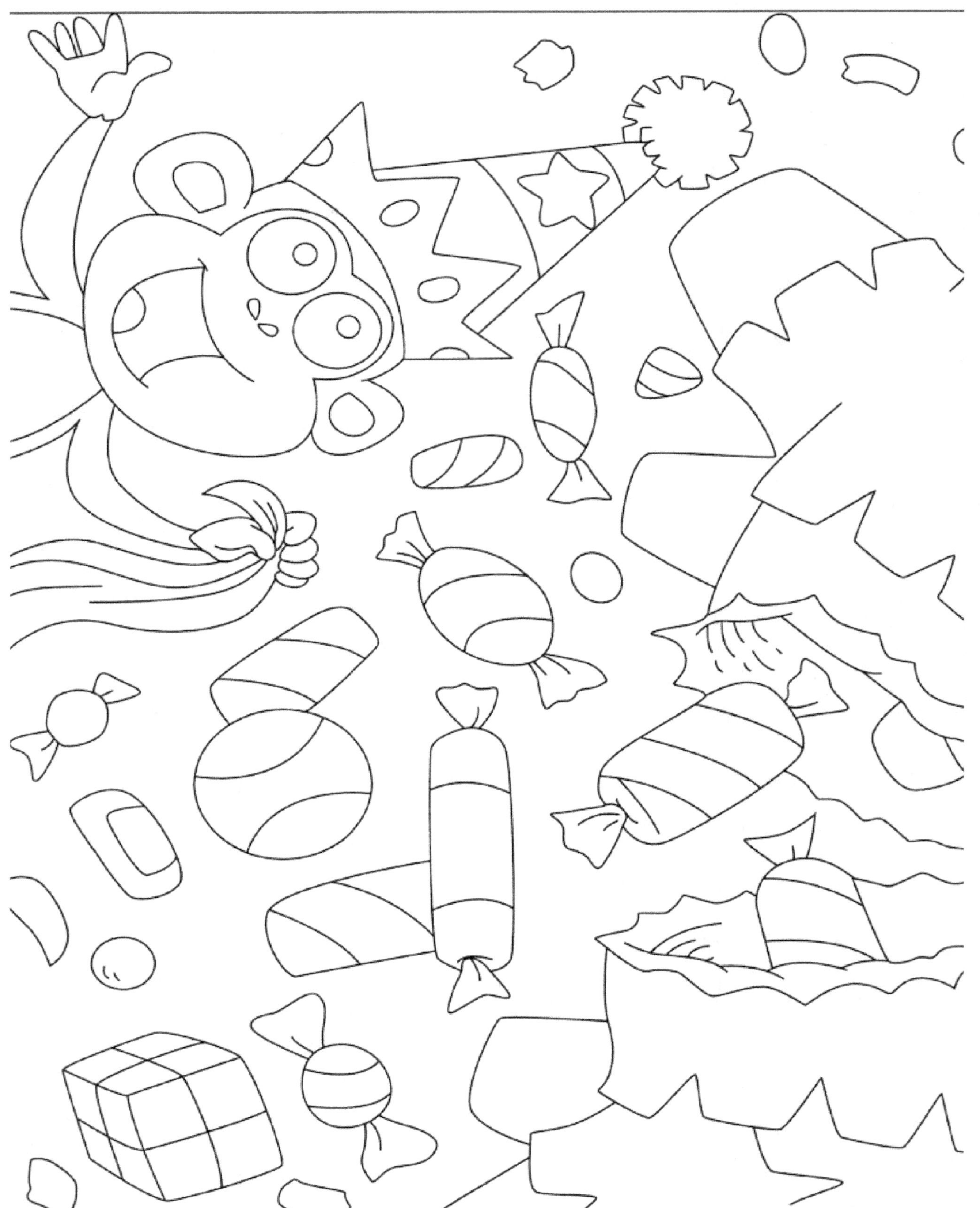

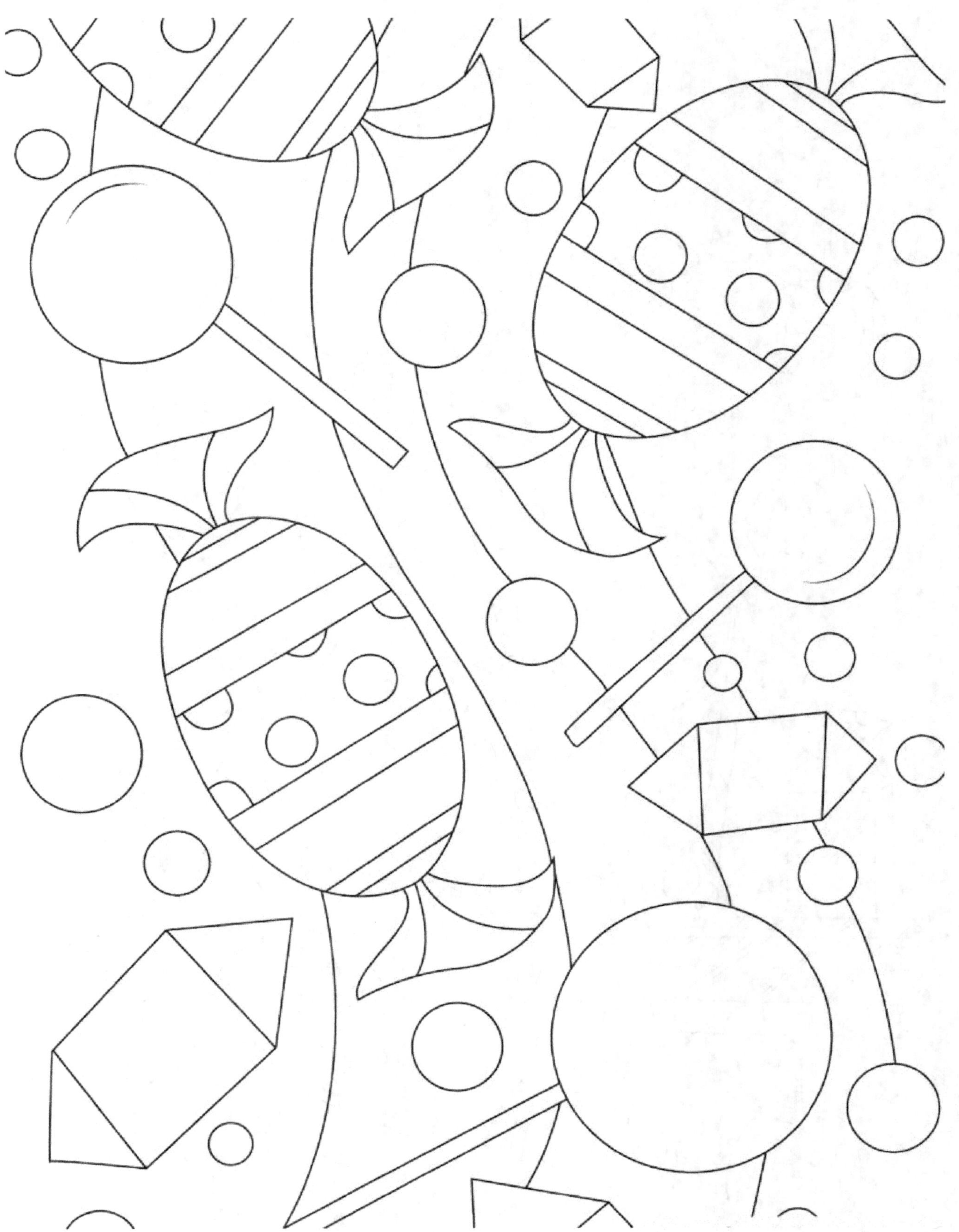

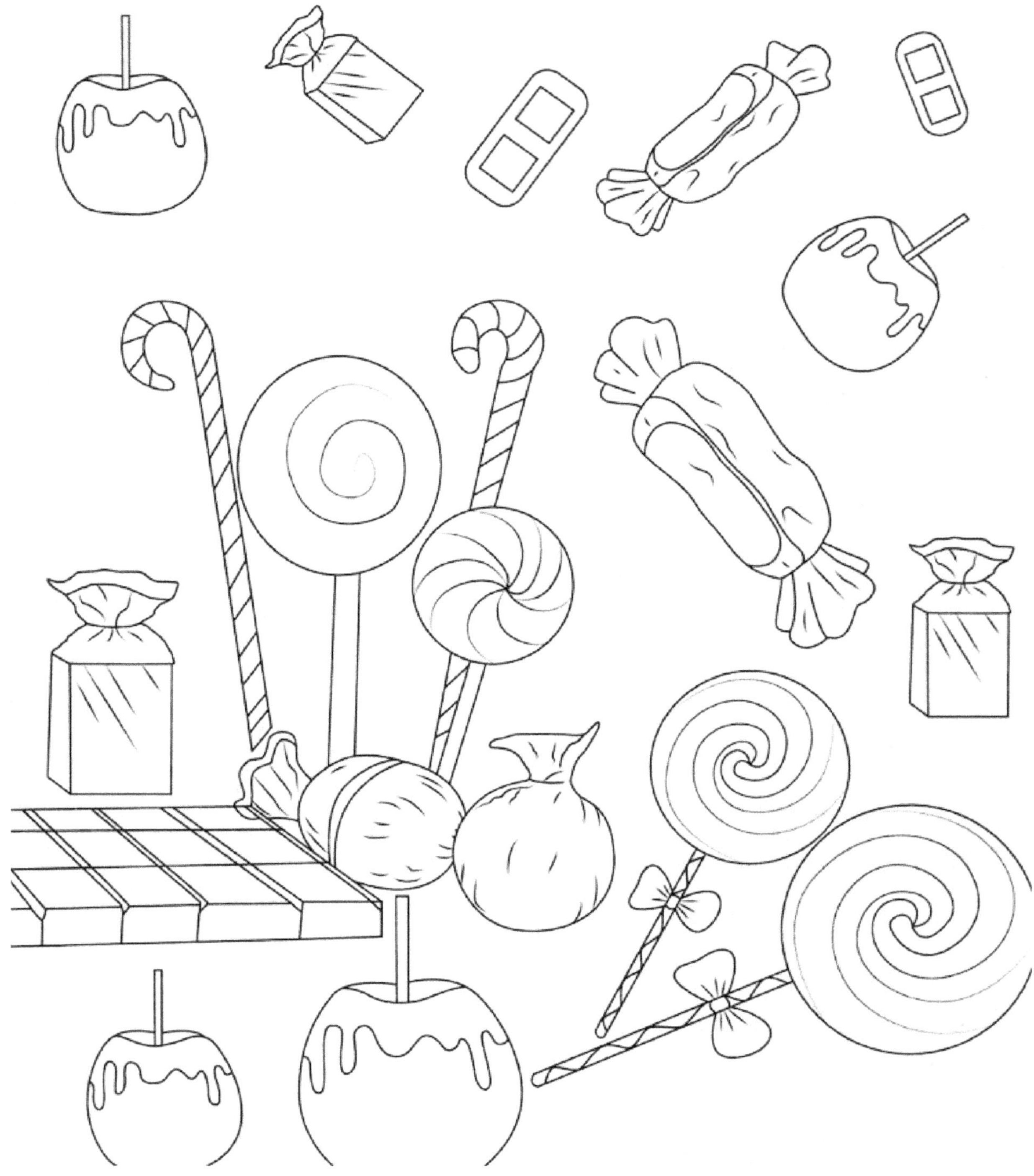

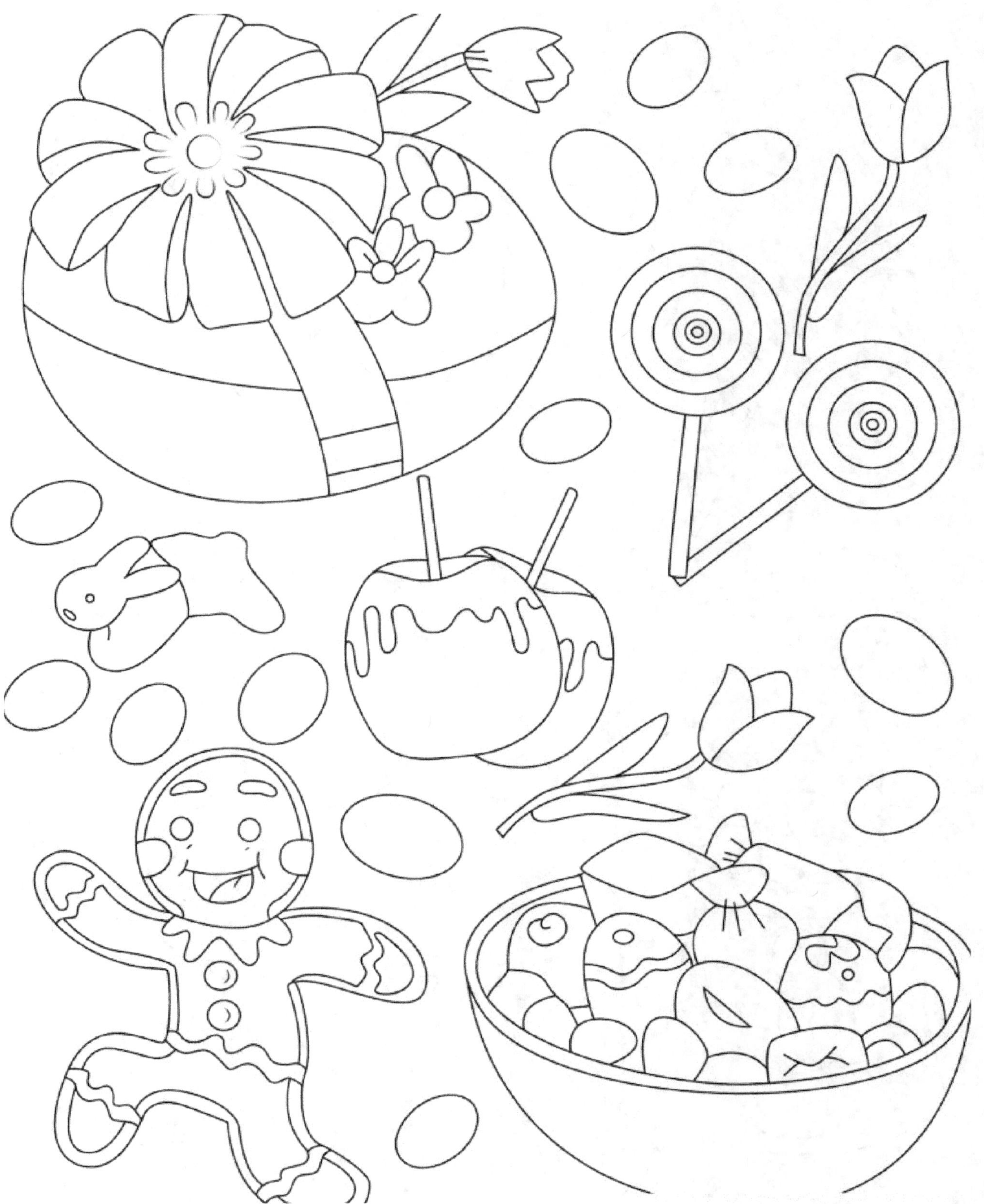

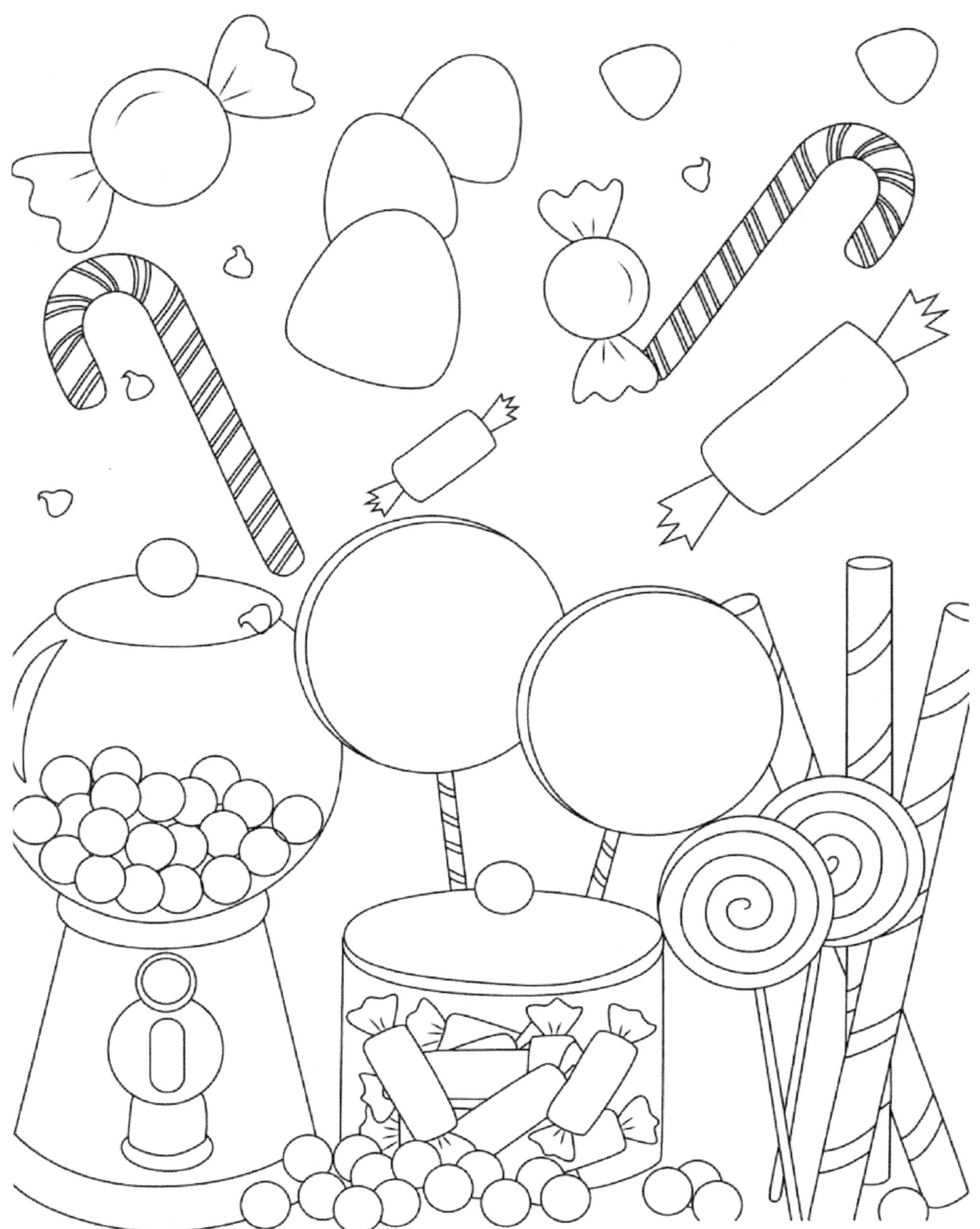

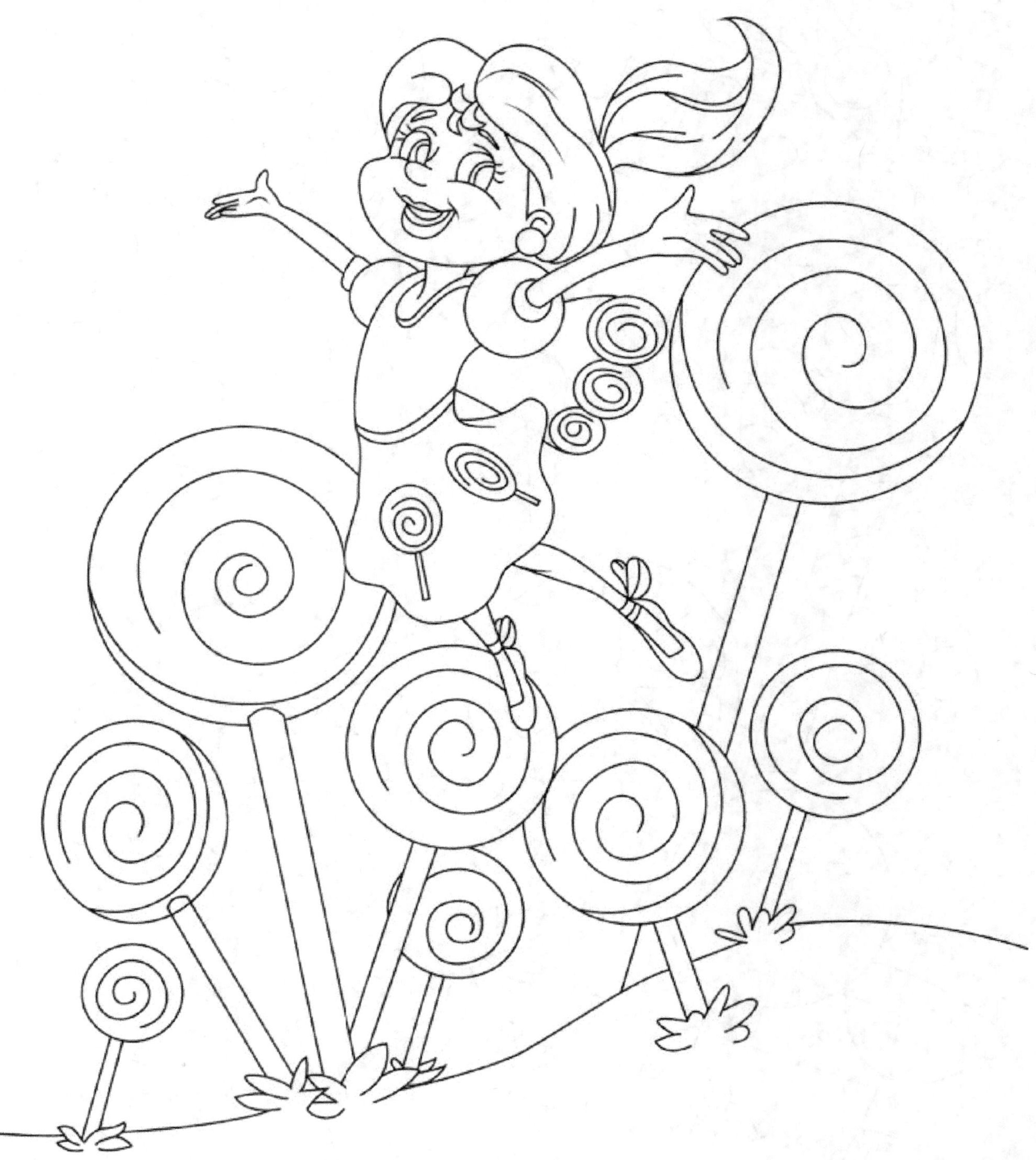

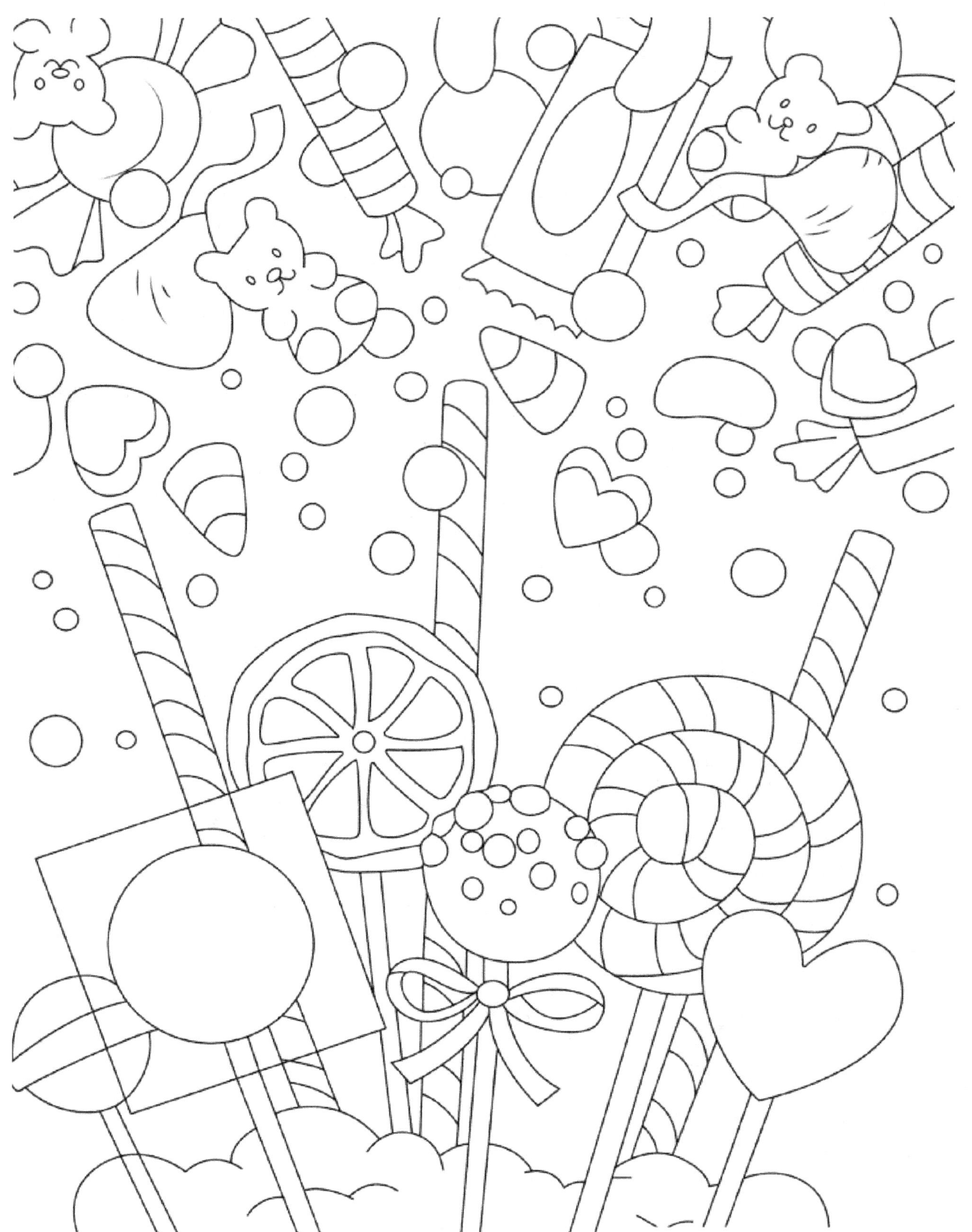

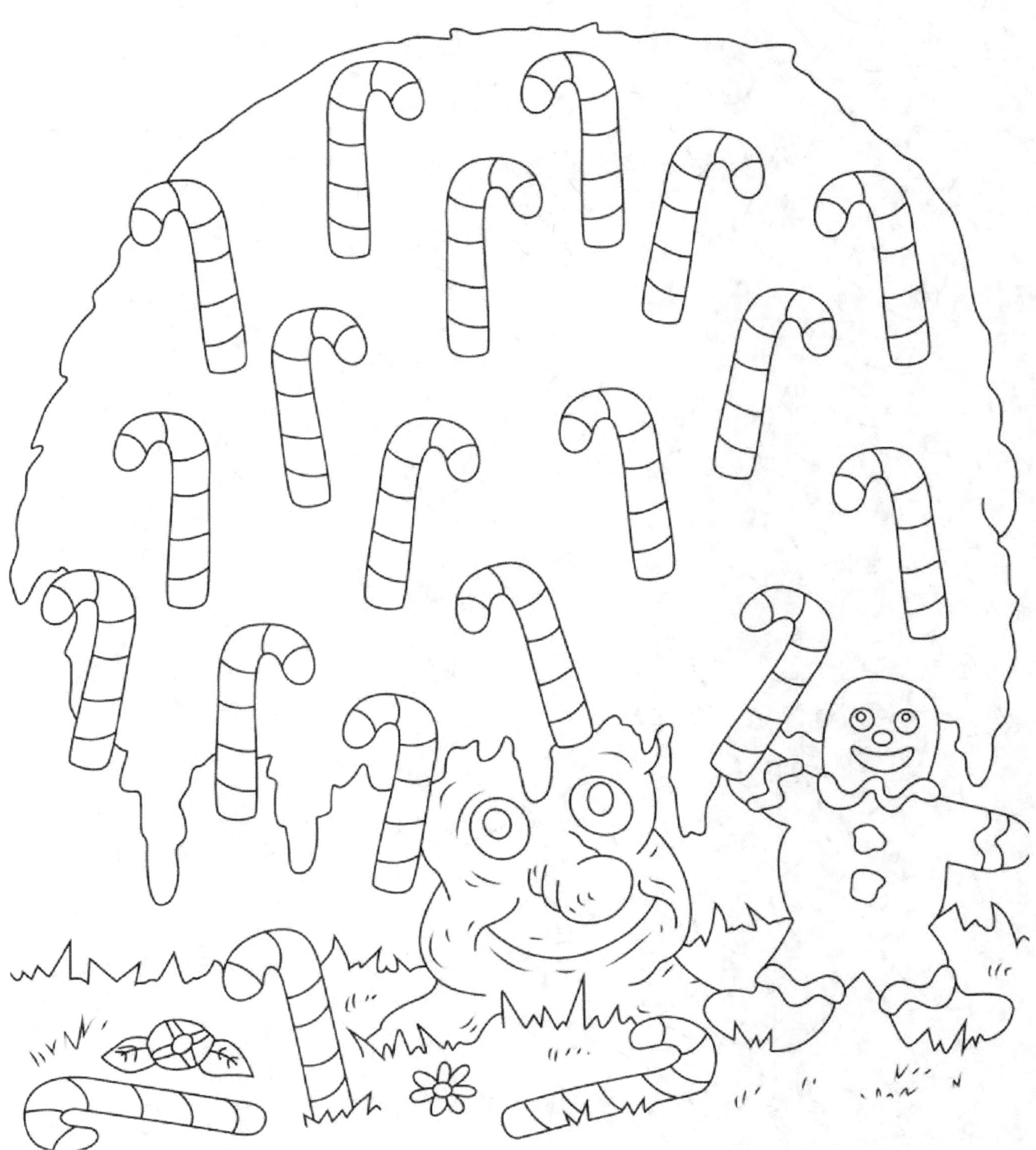

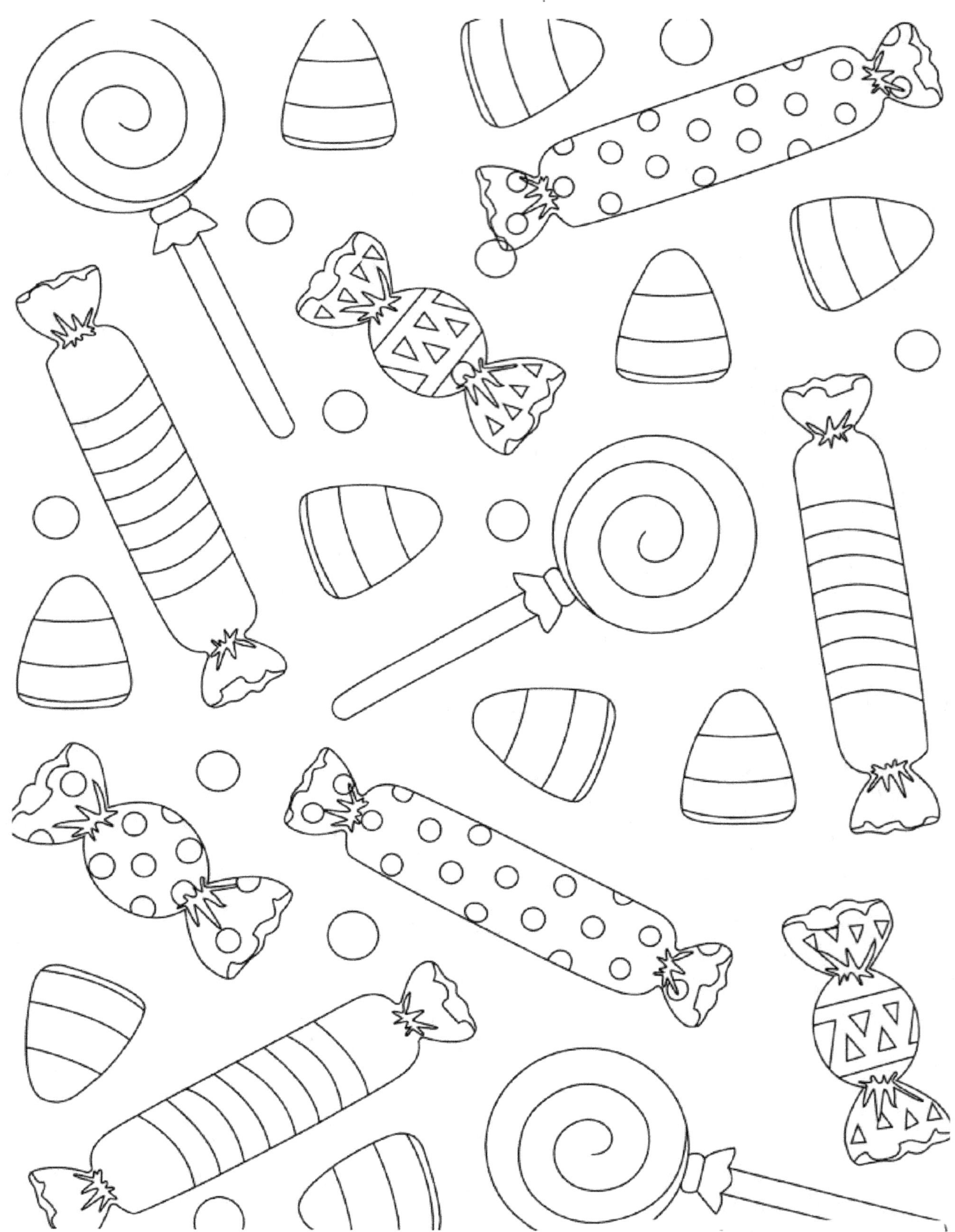

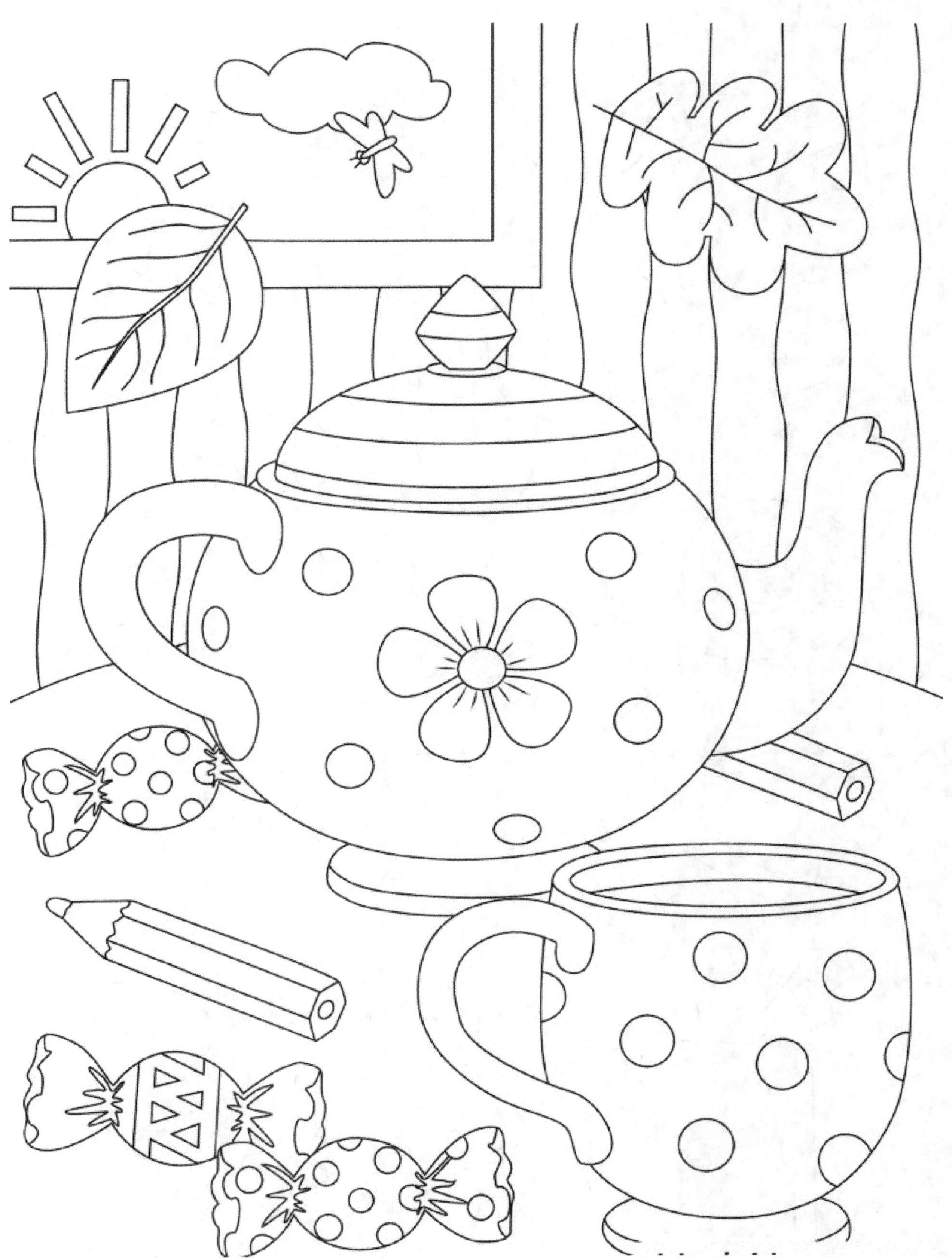

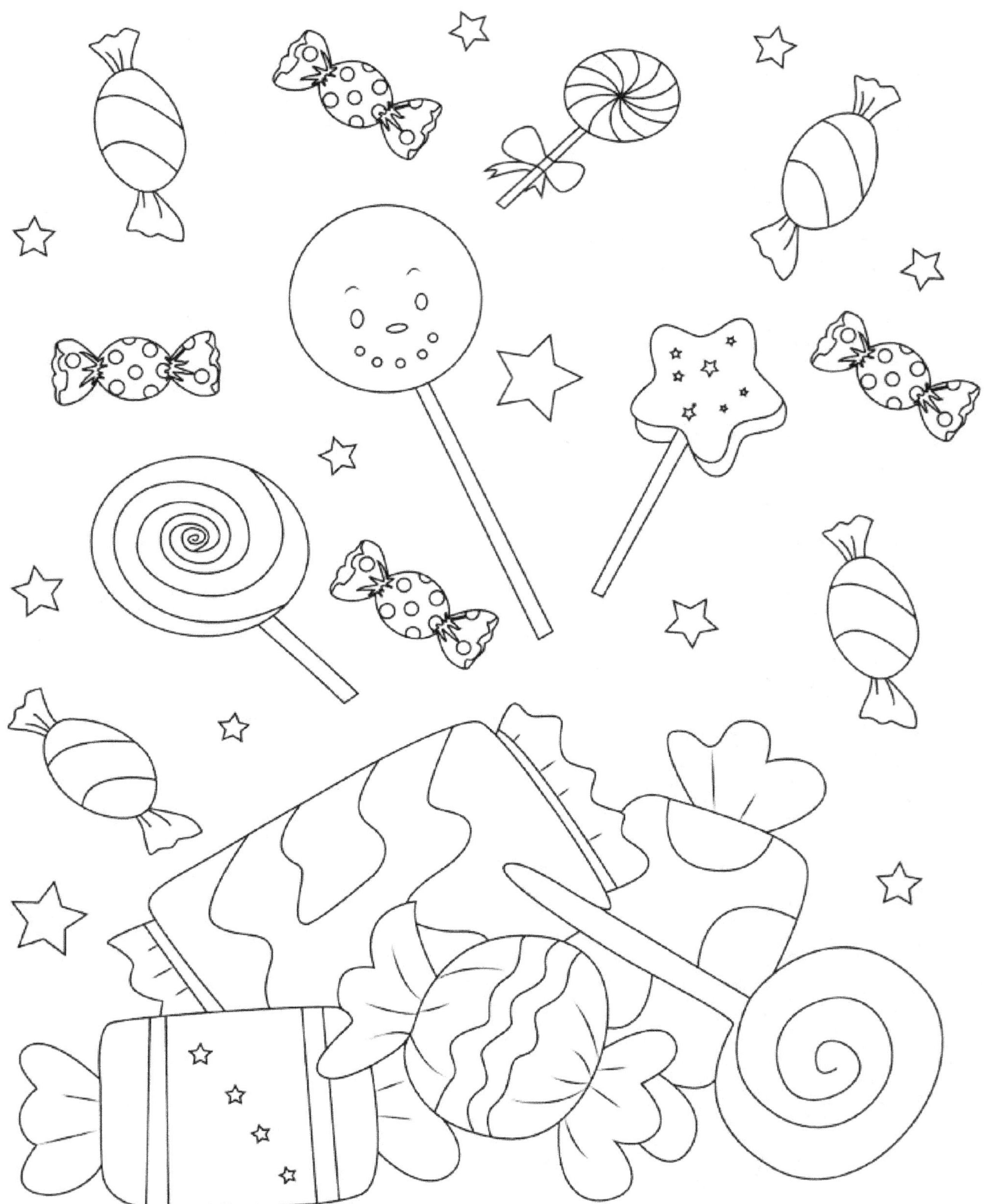

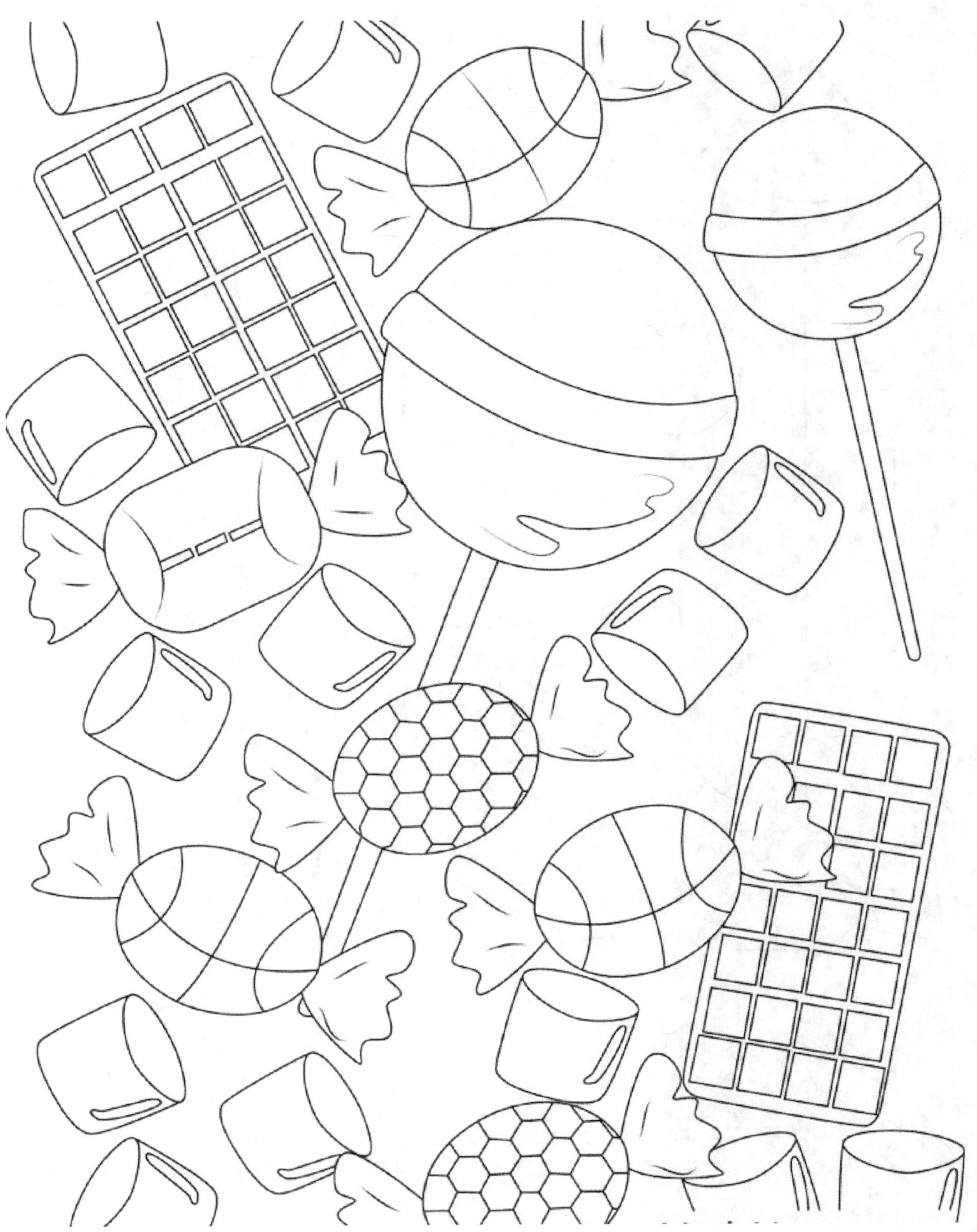

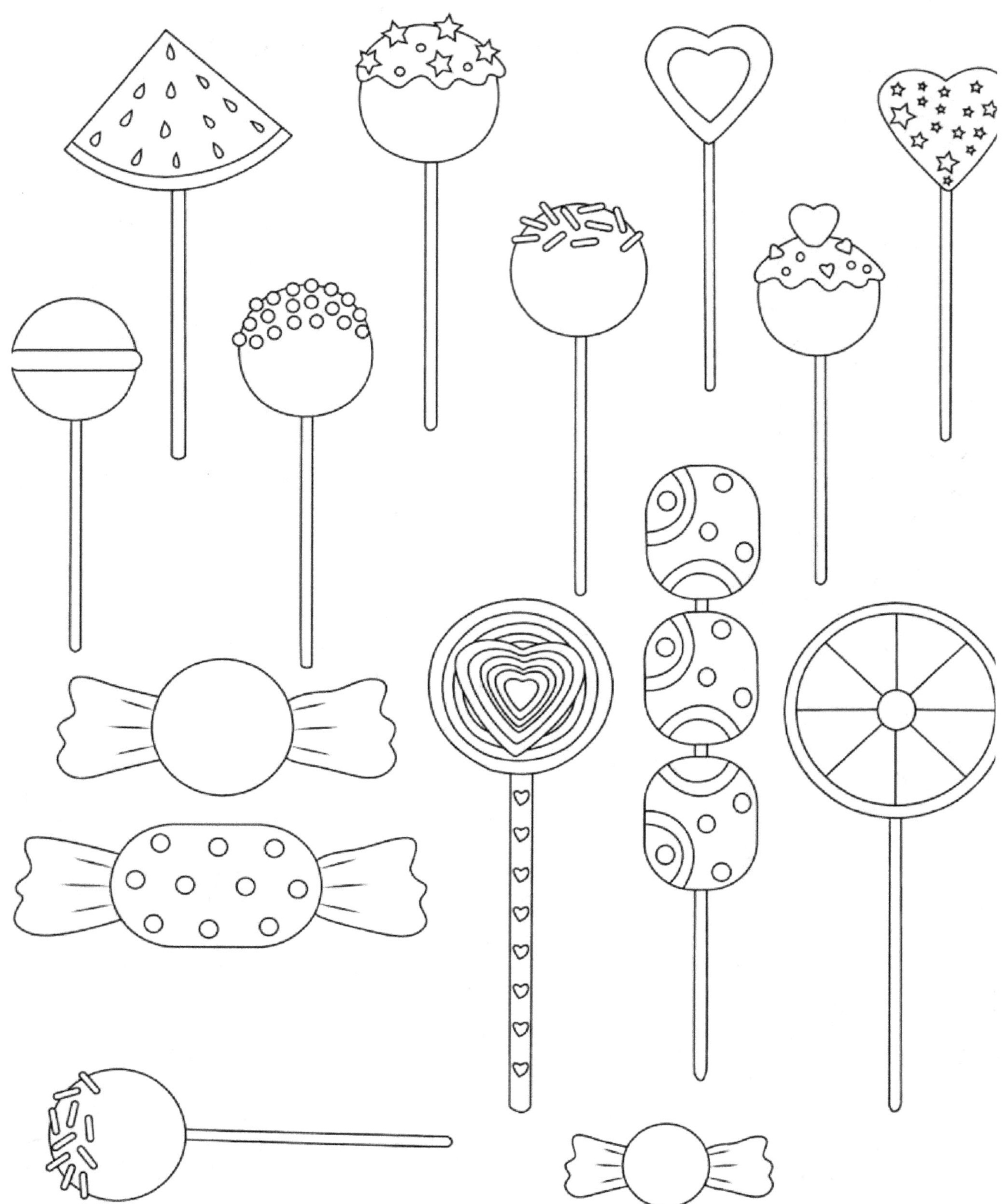

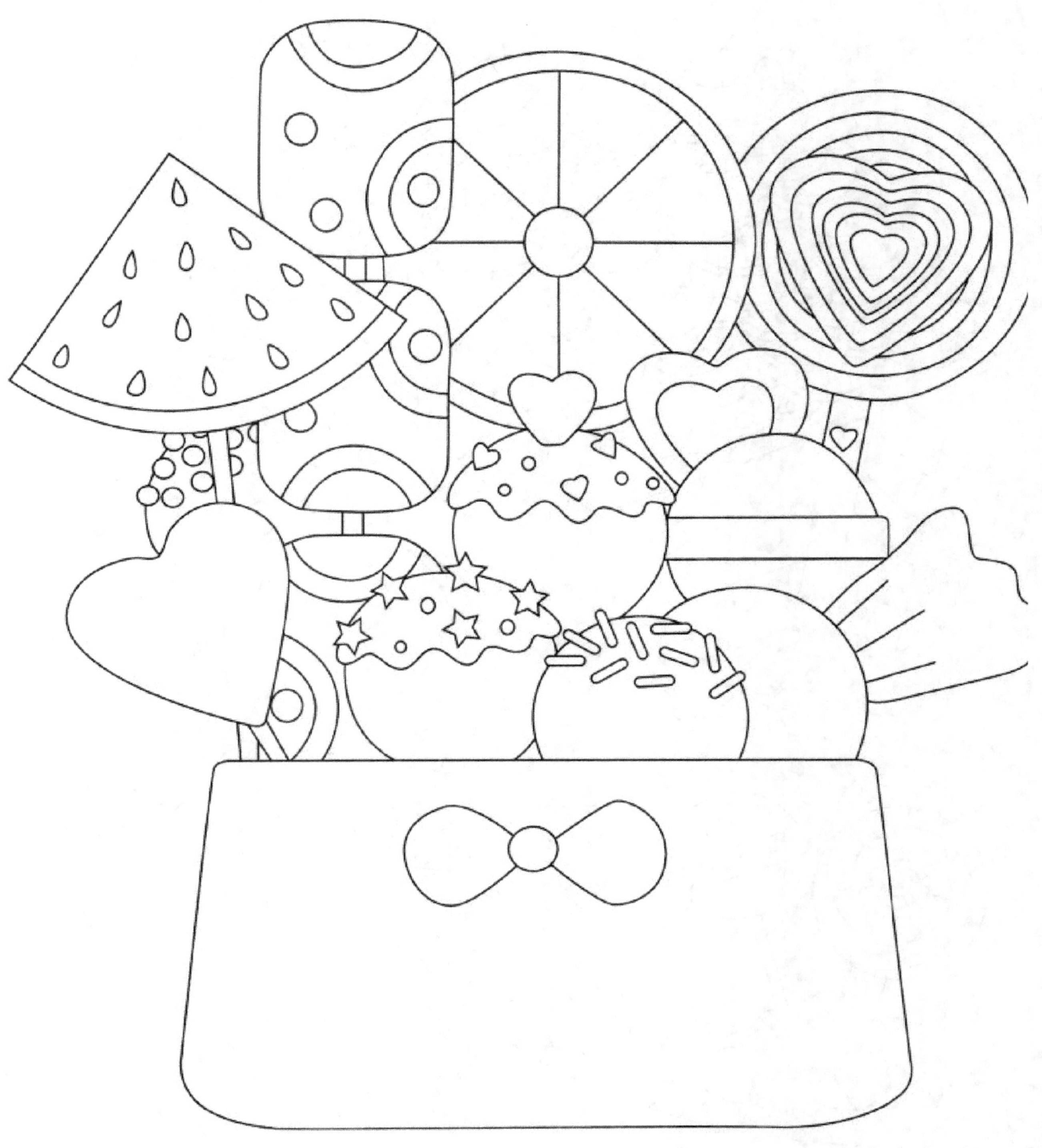

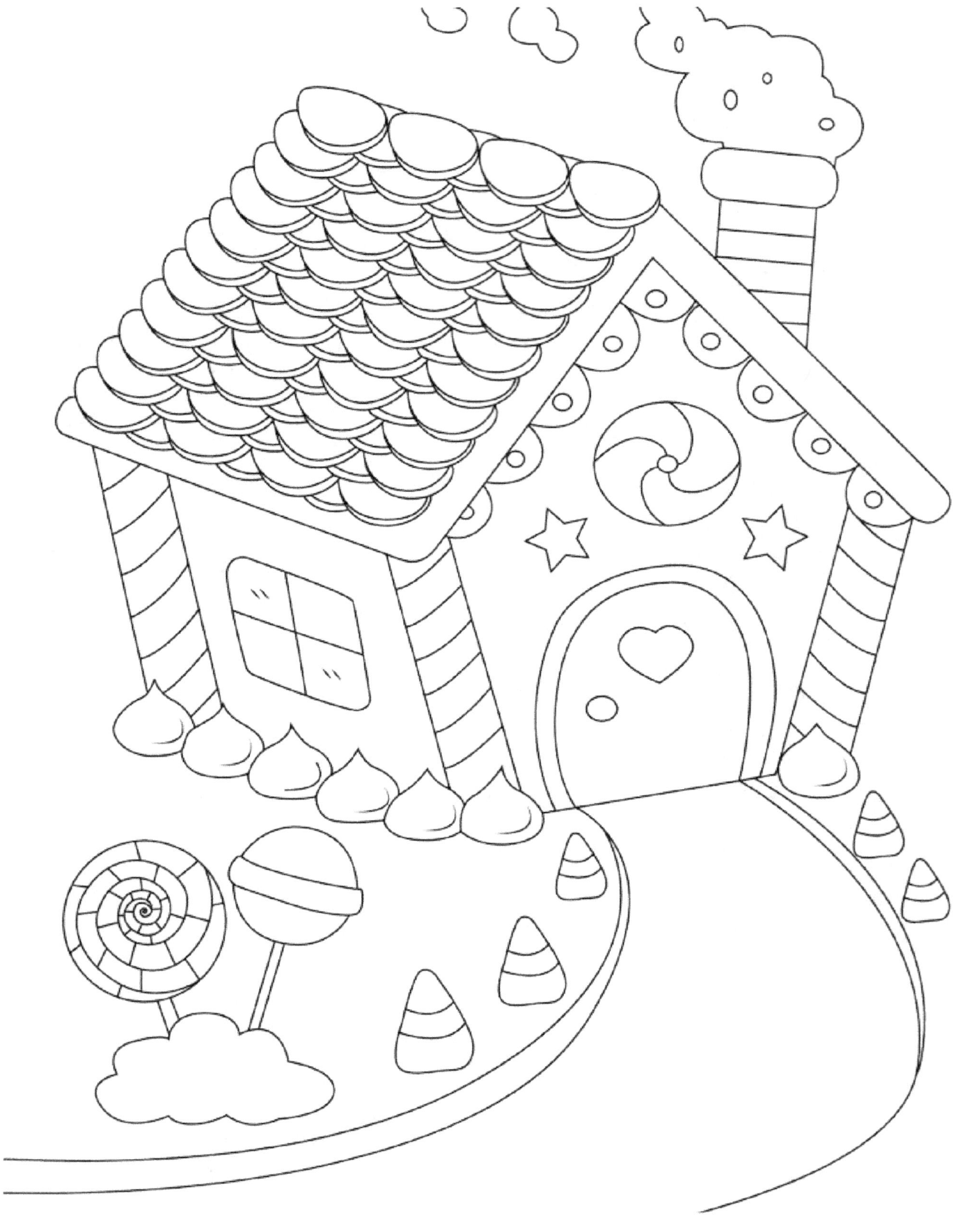

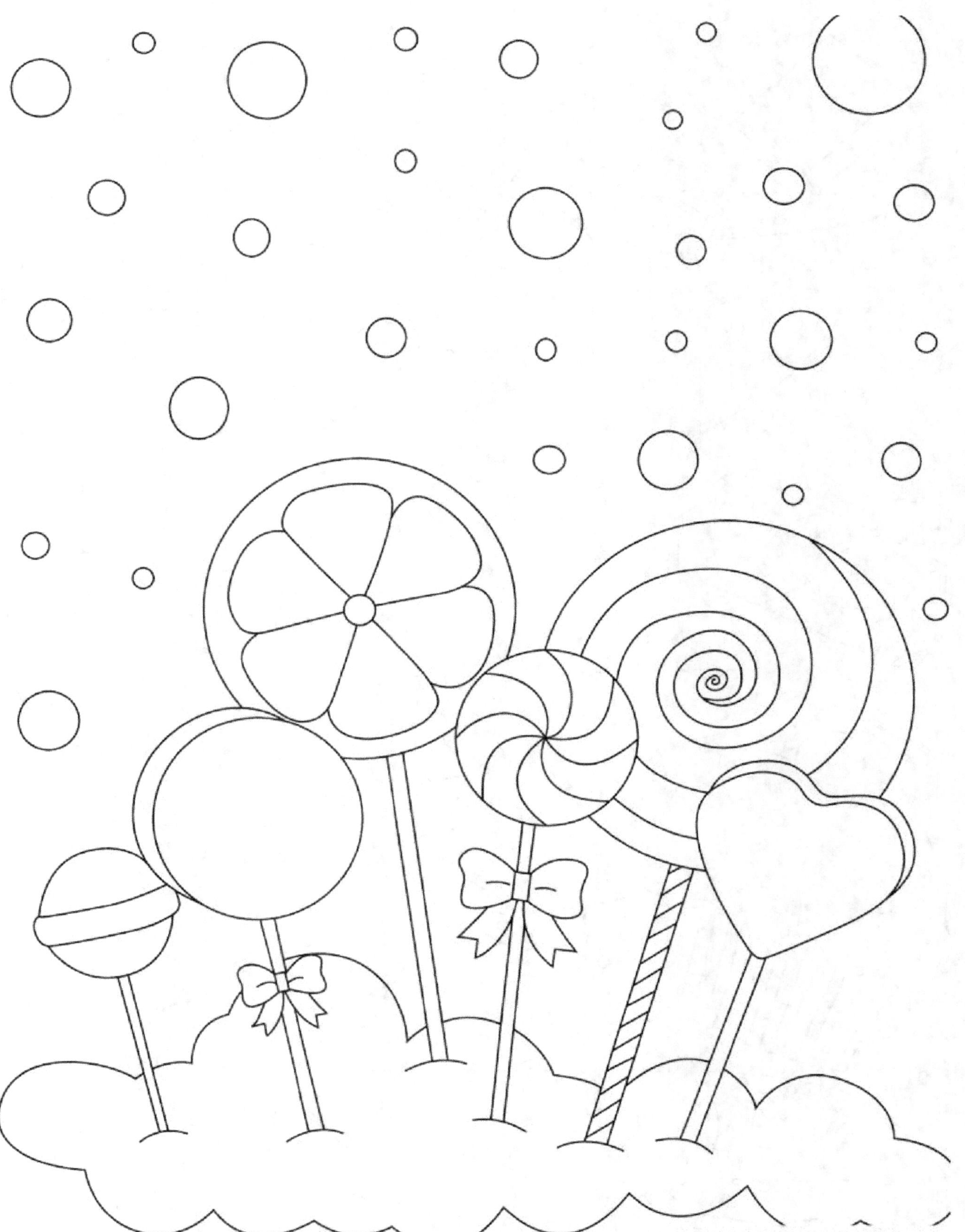

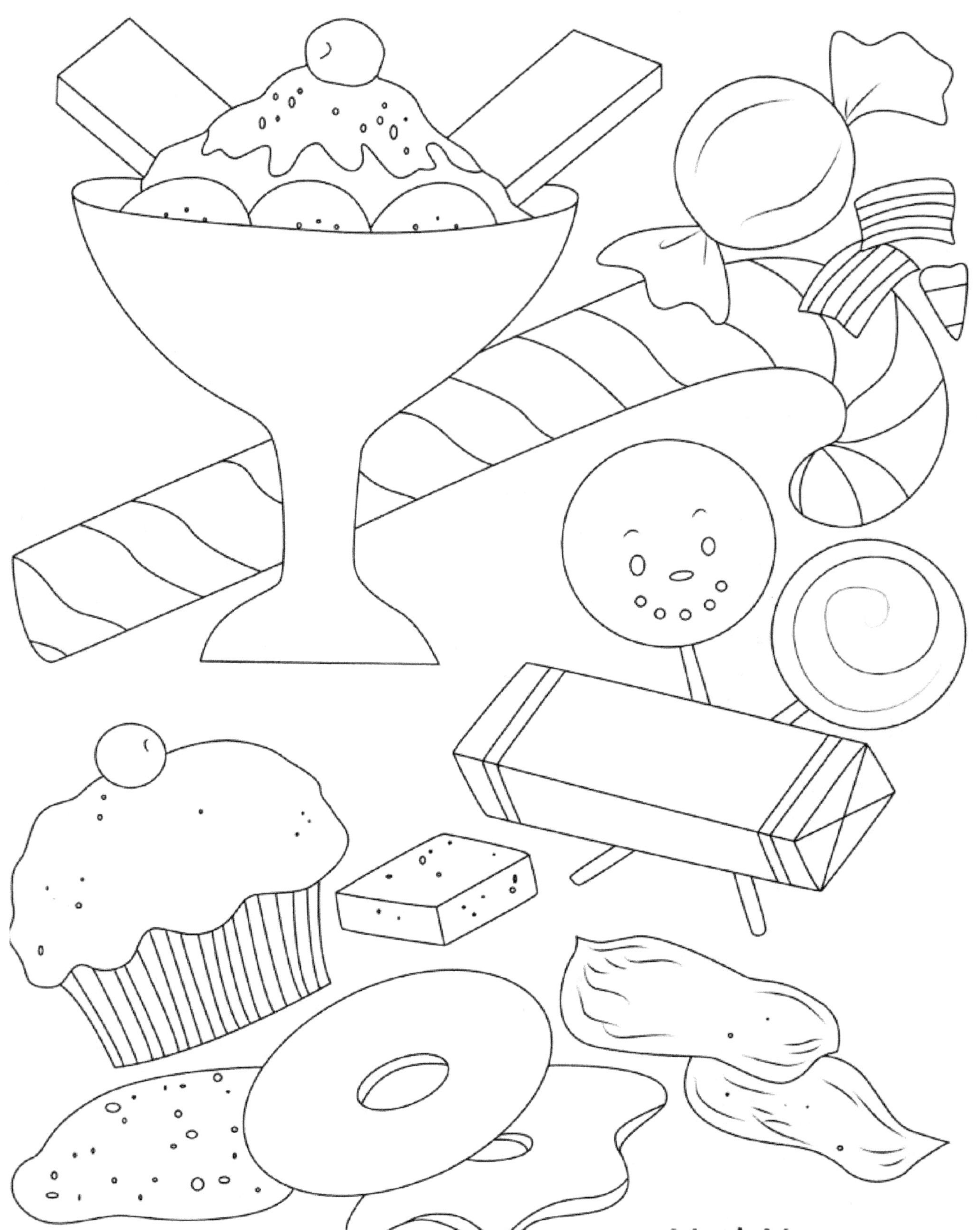

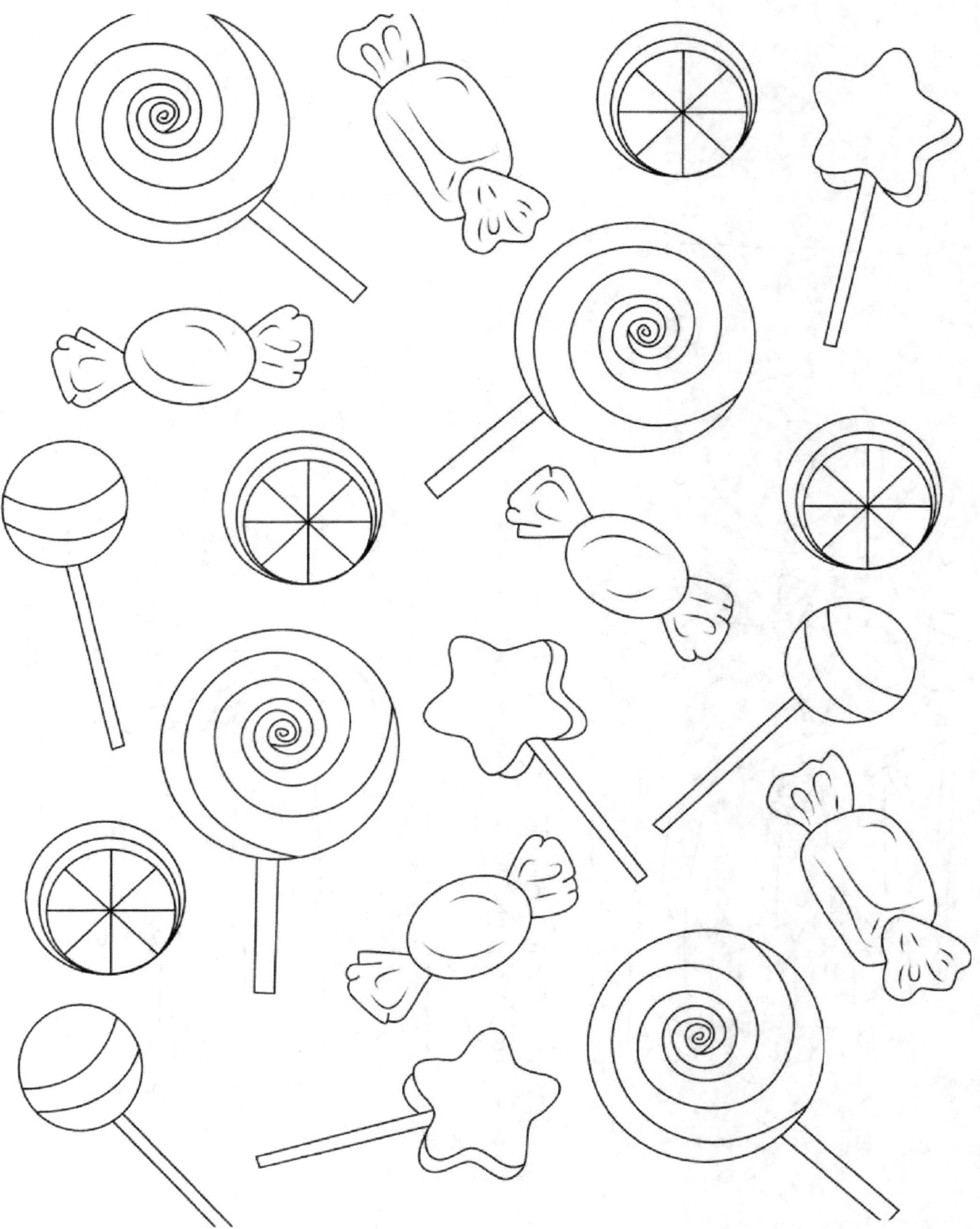

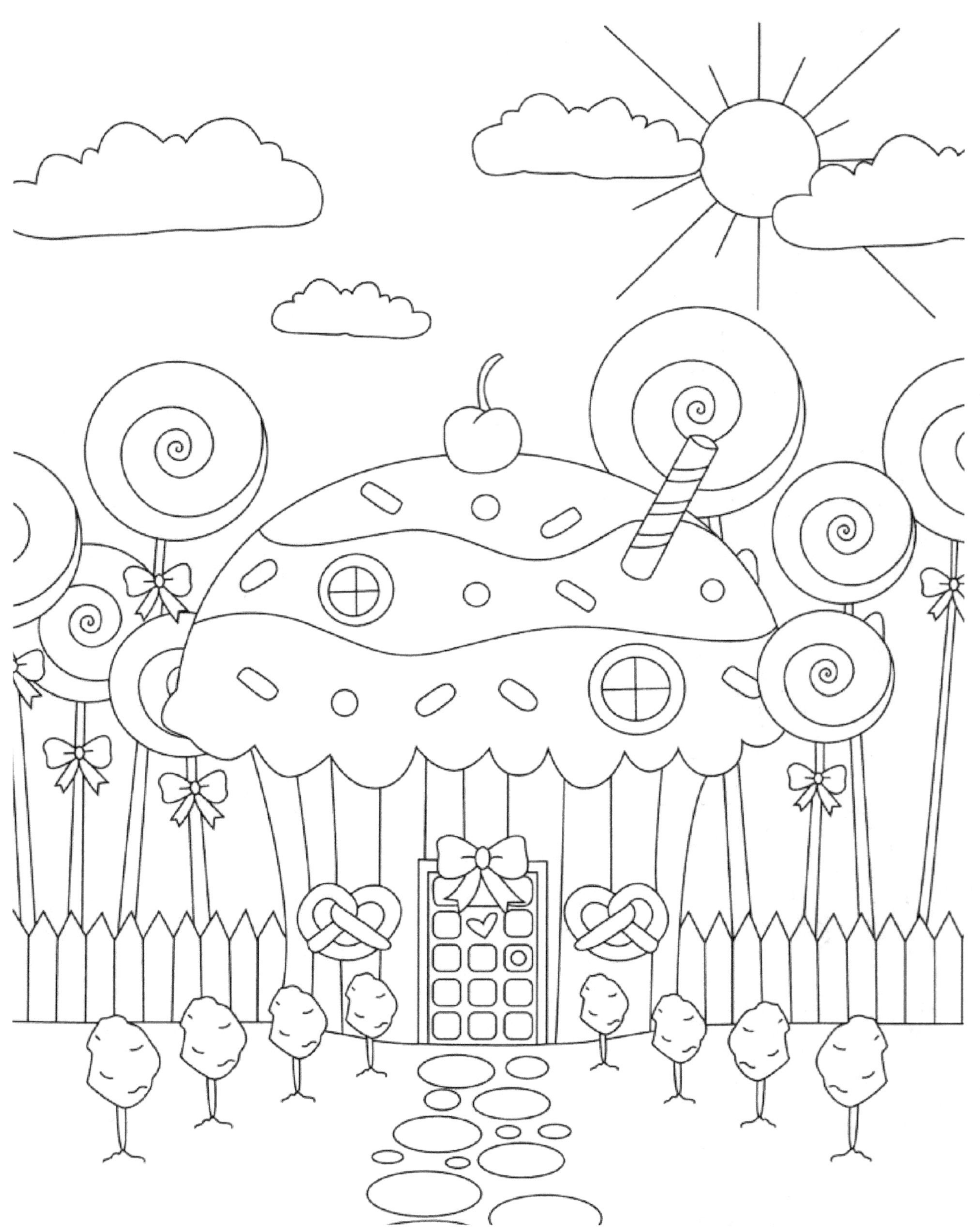

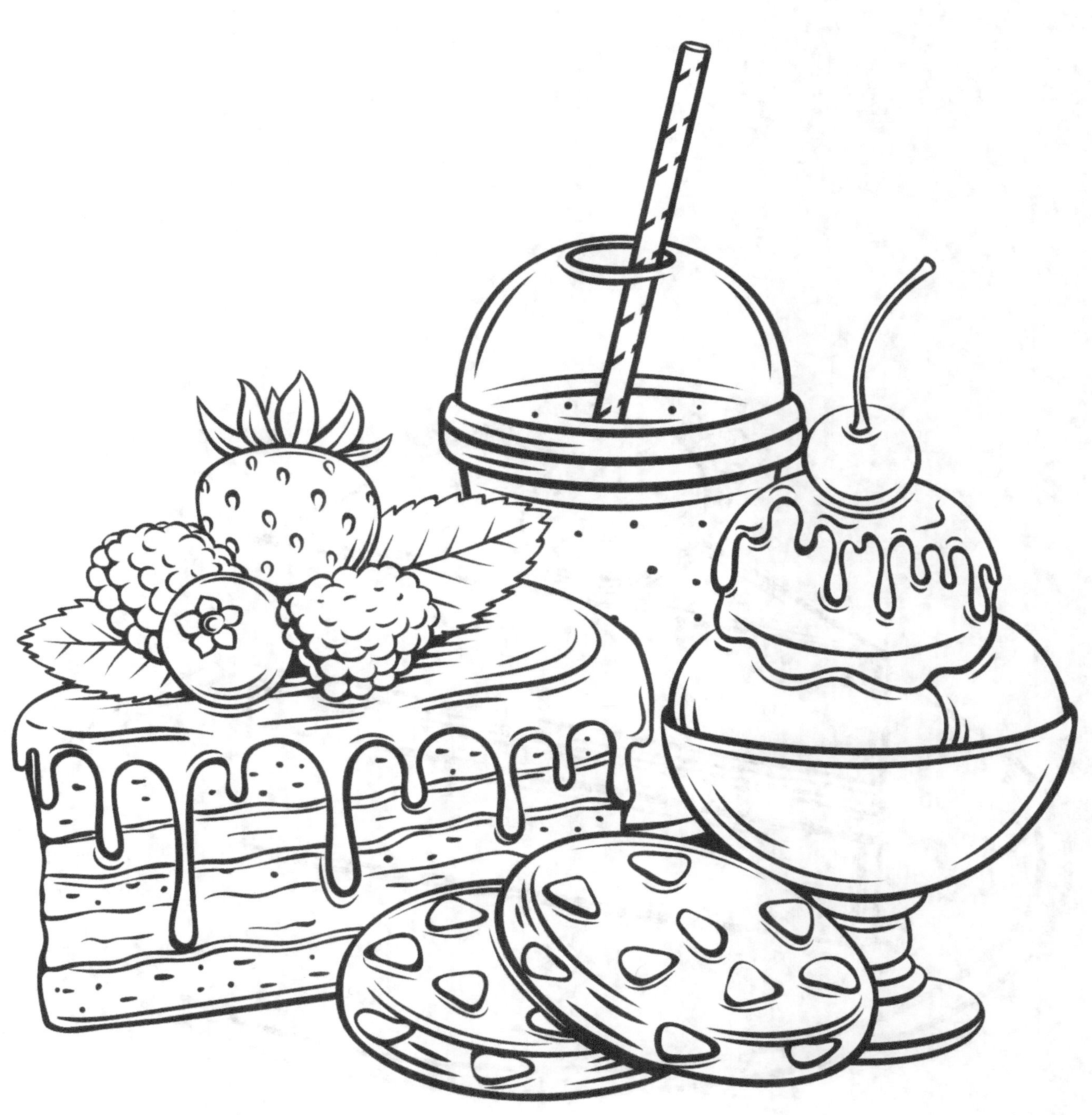

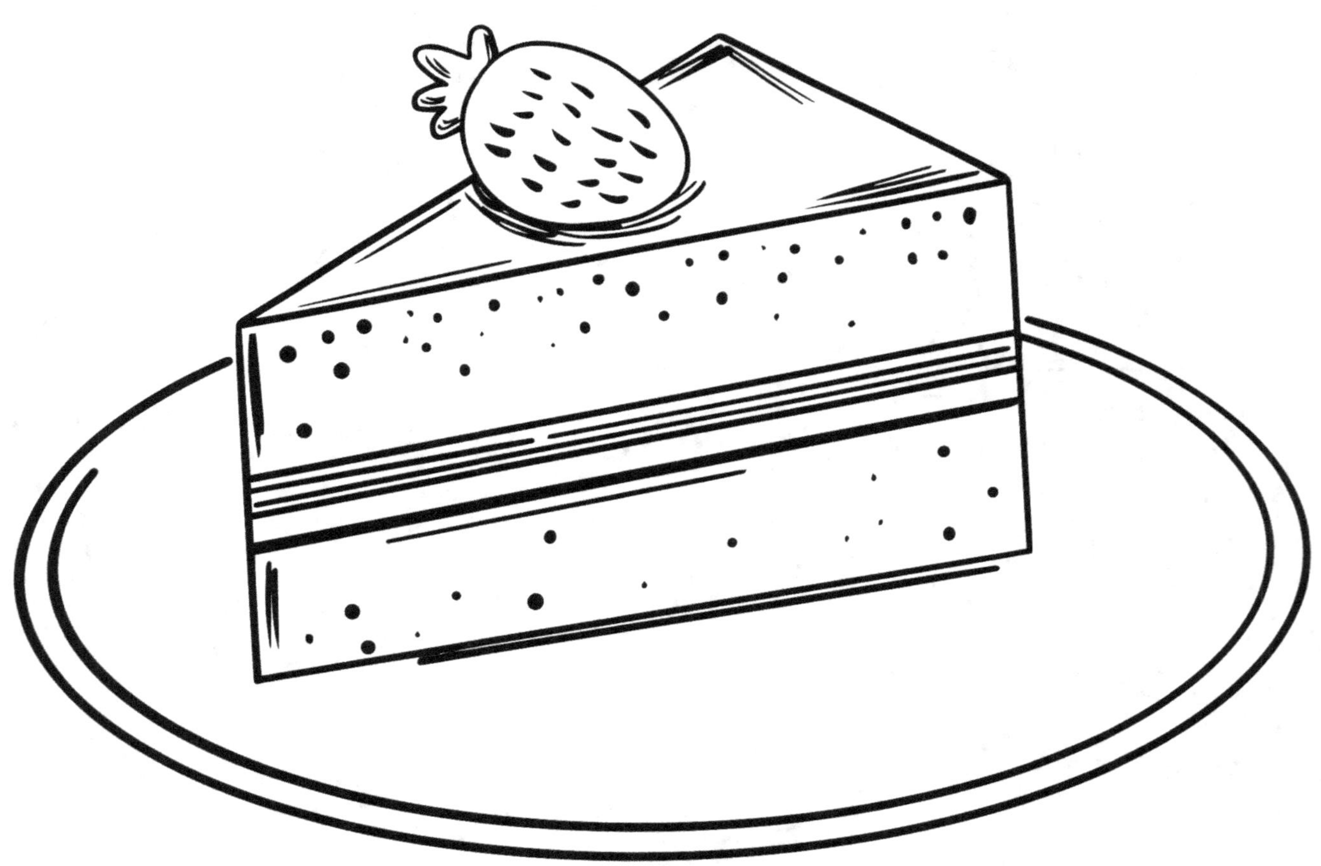

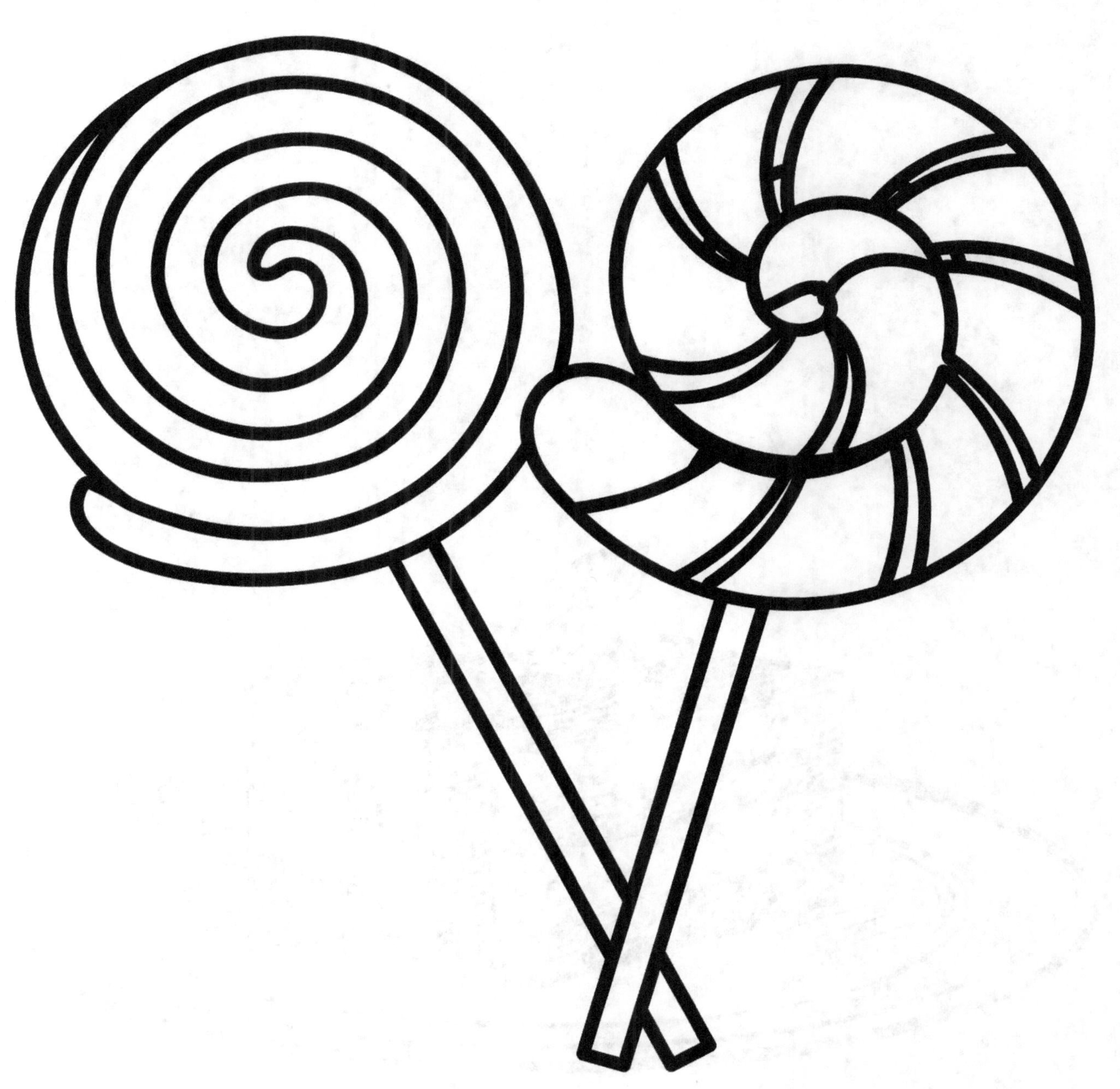

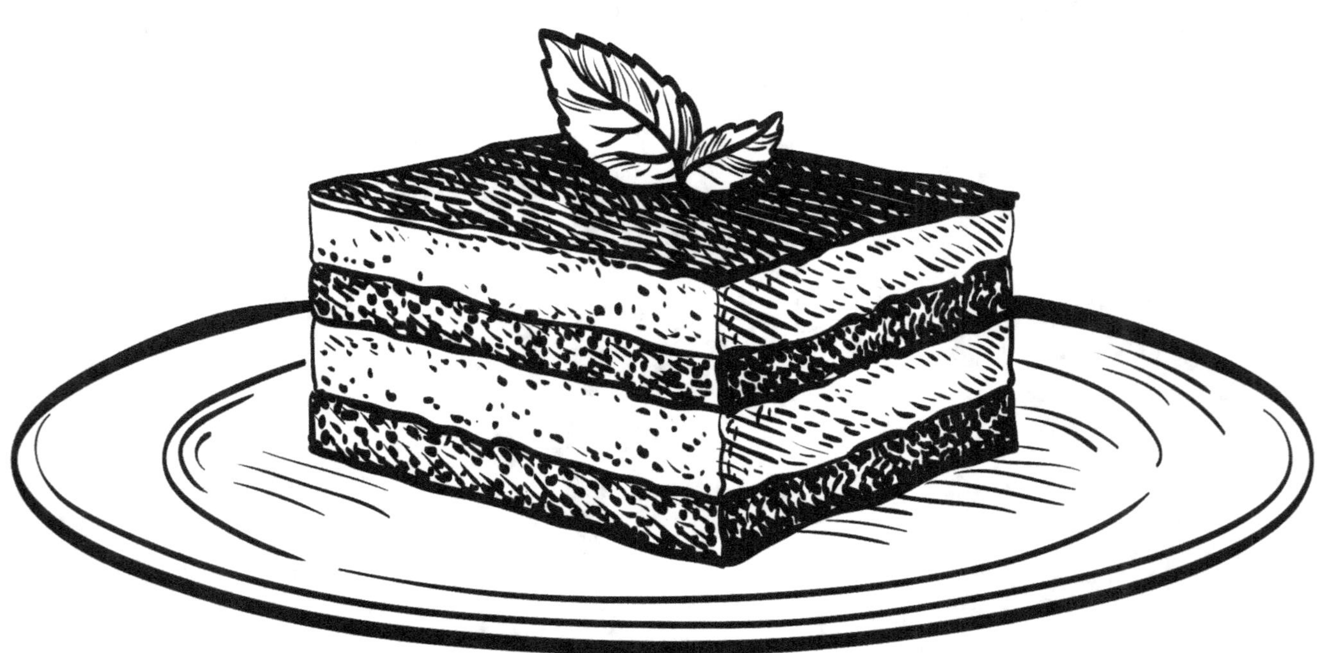

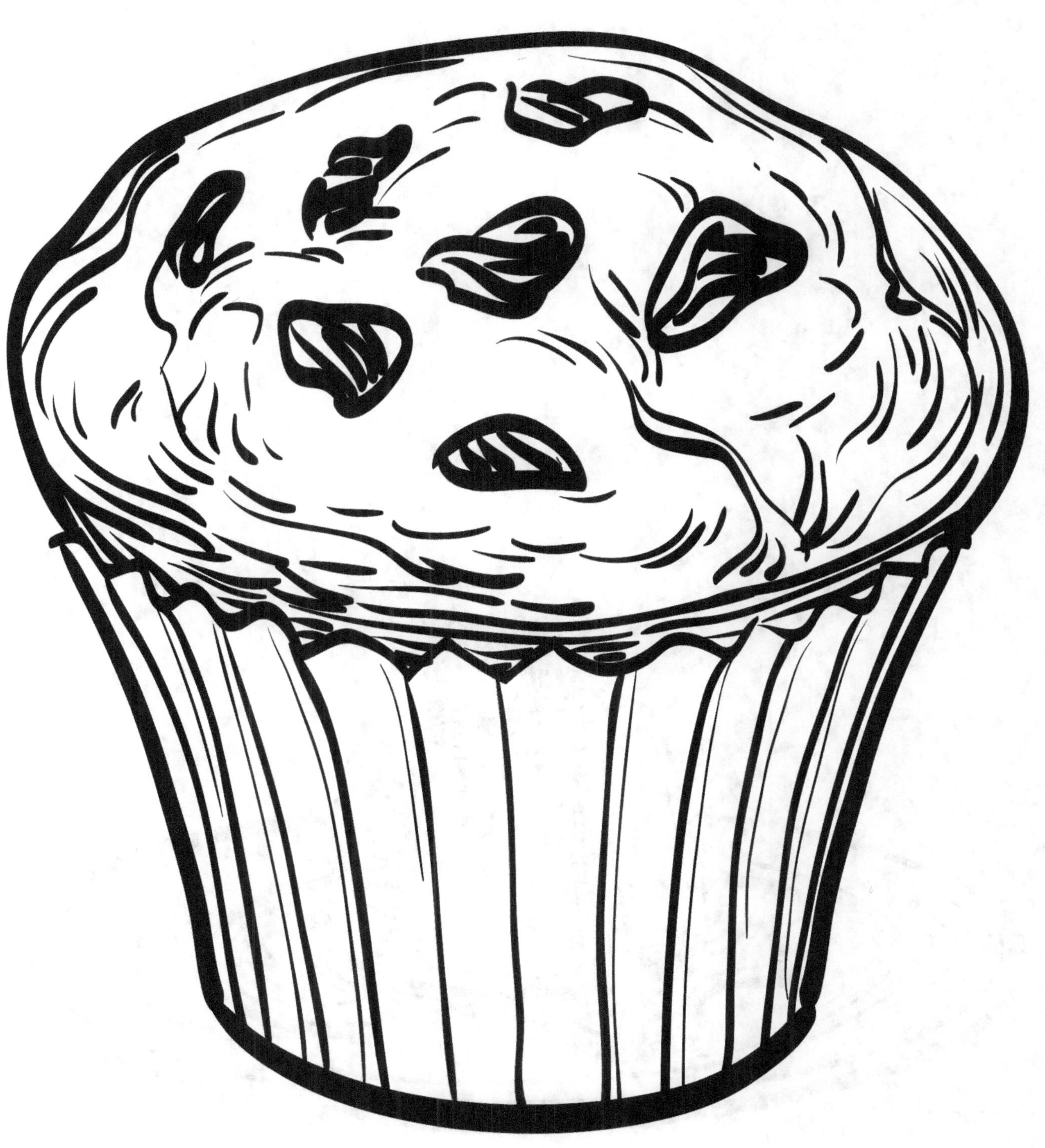

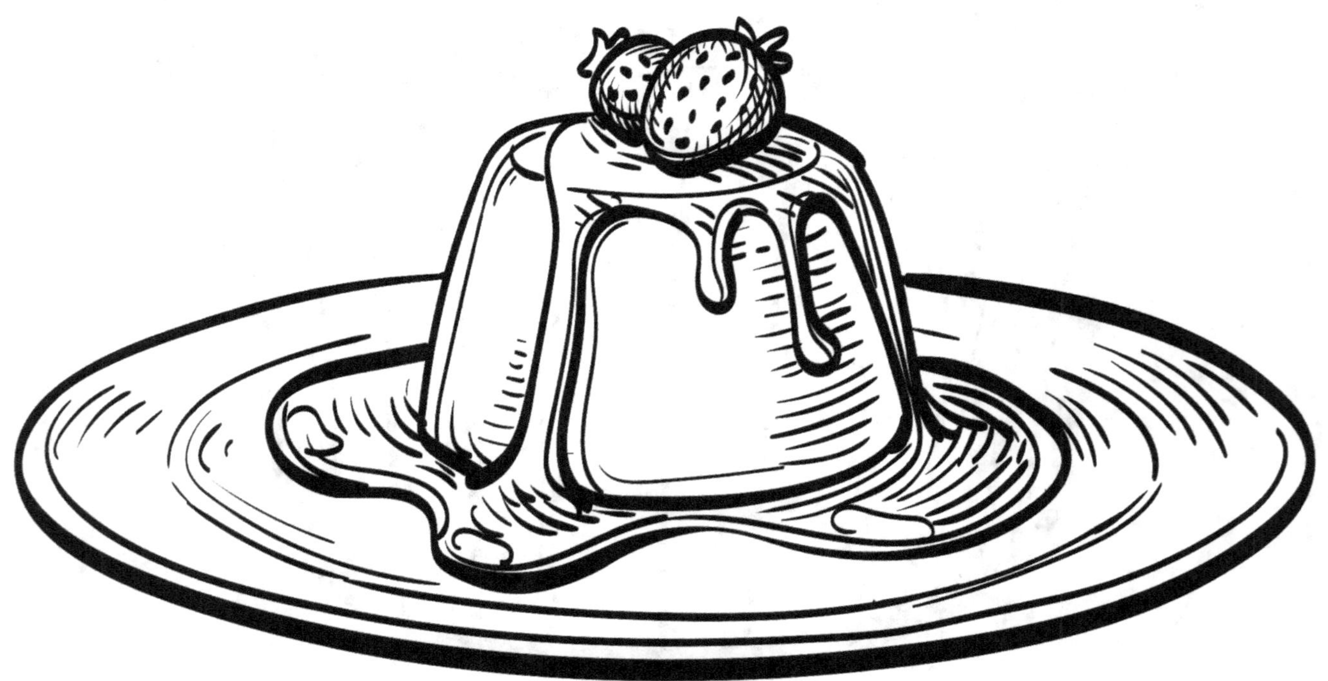

The end

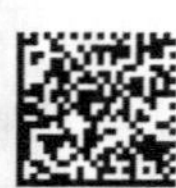

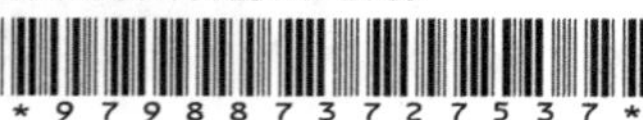
9 798873 727537